THE
SOUL
CHARGER

**ENERGIZE YOUR BEING
CONNECT WITH THE DIVINE AND CELEBRATE LIFE!**

ARCHANA S DHURANDHAR

POWERED BY

B O O K S

Author: Archana S Dhurandhar
Title: The Soul Charger
ISBN: 978-1-77204-813-1
Category: BODY, MIND & SPIRIT/Spiritual Healing

Publisher: Black Card Books
Division of Gerry Robert Enterprises Inc.
Suite 214, 5-18 Ringwood Drive
Stouffville, Ontario, Canada, L4A 0N2
International Calling: +1 877 280 8536
www.blackcardbooks.com

....

Printed in India

THE
SOUL
CHARGER

**ENERGIZE YOUR BEING
CONNECT WITH THE DIVINE AND CELEBRATE LIFE!**

ARCHANA S DHURANDHAR

POWERED BY

black card

B O O K S

TESTIMONIALS

"This is the 'missing manual' to spirituality. Archana has come through with a recipe book for the soul. Her approach to spirituality is practical and heartfelt; with this book's concise and self-contained chapters, anyone can pick it up, turn to almost any page and gain something of value from it. This is a great book, even for those who do not consider themselves particularly spiritual or religious. The advice given is not of a theological or preachy nature; it is centered on the universal tenets of peace, hope, and love."

—**Arzan Gonda,** artistic director and founder of
Rhythm India: Bollywood and Indo Fusion Dance Academy,
Houston, Texas, USA.
Master's degree in Counseling Psychology.
info@rhythm-india.com
www.rhythm-india.com

TESTIMONIALS

"*The Soul Charger* cuts straight to the chase on what you need to do to make the most of the opportunities that come your way. The author has put forth honest advice in an accessible format. This book will surely be a classic. Congratulations, Archana!"

—Ariez Tata,
President of Renaissance Jewellery Ltd.,
supporter and well-wisher
arieztataemail@gmail.com

"*The Soul Charger* is all about good thoughts, good words, and good deeds, which is the essence of all religion and beliefs and the art of healing and nurturing one's soul to reach a happy, peaceful space."

—Khush Kotwal,
genuine friend and admirer of Archana's work
khushad1@yahoo.co.in

"Author Archana S. Dhurandhar's book *The Soul Charger* is not only fantastic, but available in the hour of need. The way the author has simplified the laws of the universe is outstanding. Must-read!"

—Prem R Soni,
film director and entrepreneur
Prem@premsoni.com

"Spirituality is a necessity in today's fast-paced world. This book is beautifully written and inspires the reader to be one with the self and the universe. Every chapter ends with a positive vibe. So go ahead, connect your soul through meditation and love and experience peace and happiness in life."

—Nimesh Mehta,
author of *Sales Booster*

DEDICATION

I dedicate this book to my soul charger, Shivaay, who rekindled my passion for writing a book and helped me redefine my purpose in life. He is my source of inspiration, my guardian angel, my anchor, my mentor, and my best critic, who has lifted my spirits and given me the needed boost to rise and shine in the most crucial circumstances and seasons of life. He has been my pillar of strength all through the journey of my first book with his divine presence, and the journey continues...

ACKNOWLEDGMENTS

Om Namah Shivaay!

The journey of *The Soul Charger* was sparked with a thought of self-realization about pursuing my burning passion to write my own book, a thought I had shelved during the grind of daily life. From this point on, the universe manifested my thoughts to reality in its mysterious ways by getting me associated with Gerry Robert and the team at Black Card Books (BCB) with my college buddy, Nimesh Mehta. I soon realized that this was what I always wanted to do: Write my own book. I took a step forward following my instincts with the support of my inner circle, who kept their faith in my ability and commitment to make my dream come true. There were many who questioned my decision, ability, and commitment towards my book. I thank them the most, as they galvanized me to give my 200% to make this happen.

It is my privilege to publish my first book under the flagship of BCB. The entire book journey has been very eventful, full of challenging situations on the personal front, including sporadic health breakdowns and a road accident that paused my flow of thoughts momentarily. However, with the blessings of the divine and the support of my family, inner circle, and well-wishers, I have continued to charge my soul and have emerged stronger. I guess I had to pass through these testing times to add meaning to every thought and word I penned.

ACKNOWLEDGMENTS

I am blessed to be a part of The Brahma Kumaris World Spiritual University to nourish my thoughts with a daily potion of godly knowledge—*Murli*—and energize my soul by connecting with the divine through *Rajyoga* meditation. All the members of this spiritual family have been very appreciative and have extended their selfless support and guidance in the making of my book.

I am so humbled and touched by the kind words of encouragement and appreciation for my book from Bk Sister Shivani, whom I admire and follow. She was the first divine soul to browse through the content and bless the draft manuscript of *The Soul Charger* in December 2017, when I had the opportunity to meet her at a spiritual seminar in Mumbai.

The love and blessings showered by my deceased and living grandparents, my parents (Suren and Minal), my sister (Kavita), my brother-in-law (Pavan), my family, my little nephews (Parjnya and Vedant), friends, and well-wishers have kept me going. I am grateful to Mr. Zarine Randeria and my Reiki teacher Mrs. Anjali Sengupta for their continued love, support, and divine protection. I am thankful to Shruti Tejwani and her team for giving a facelift to my outlook with their professional grooming and photography. Thank you, Dr. Nilesh Sawant, for taking care of my physical and emotional health and always being there for me as a well-wisher, friend, and guide. I am privileged to work with the Creations family, who has given me the required personal space and peace to pursue my passion alongside my career.

A special thanks to all my well-wishers for the testimonials and the seven special souls who were destined to be a part of my book to elevate its vibrations with their presence and the shared knowledge in the excerpts of their interviews. Thank you for your valuable time and words of wisdom. Lastly, I express my heartfelt gratitude to my cousin Roma Malik for her consistent support, encouragement, guidance, and help in refining the content of my book. She not only made time to work with me on my book in spite of her responsibilities, but she also helped me gather myself and lift my spirits to hold my pen and nudged me to complete my book. The journey of my soul to *The Soul Charger* has only been possible with the blessings of the Supreme Power and all the divine souls who have contributed to my book in their own special way. *Om Shanti.*

TABLE OF CONTENTS

INTRODUCTION

The Soul Charger is a godly message that I wish to convey to all the beautiful souls on this planet, on behalf of the Supreme Soul. I consider myself as his conch shell, through which I have made a humble attempt to spread the music of His divine knowledge. I acquired this knowledge through the journey of my life and experiences. This also includes the thoughts shared by the enlightened souls whose work I have read and whom I have heard and met on life's pathway, especially all my teachers and mentors at Eckaankur Holistic Healing, where I was initiated as a Reiki channel, and the Brahma Kumaris World Spiritual University, where I learned Rajyoga meditation.

I continue to seek the godly knowledge of the Supreme Power as a student and part of this wonderful spiritual family who have influenced, transformed, and refined my thoughts, belief system, and attitude towards life. Nevertheless, I am grateful to each and every soul that has stepped into my life, for a season or a reason, and who has had something to contribute, inspire, encourage, motivate, empower, and enable me to pen down my thoughts in my first book, *The Soul Charger*.

Before you read the chapters to follow, I have tried to simplify here the basic concepts of *Rajyoga* that revolve around the core content of the book for an easier and better connection.

Spirituality is a conscious move to connect with the divine. It's the study and understanding of:

- The Soul (*Atma*)
- The Supreme Soul (*Paramatma*)

1

- Time *(Samay)*
- Karmic Cycle *(Karma)*

Spirituality introduces us to the three important aspects of life.

- Who am I?
- Where did I come from?
- Where am I going?

When we draw the sketch of a human body, do we draw the mind? No! Because we cannot see it like our other body parts and we do not feel its significance in our life. But there is an energy that drives our body. What is this energy? Where does it come from? And what is its source?

What Is a Soul?

A Soul is a **S**ource **O**f **U**nique point of **L**ight. It is different from the body and the brain. The soul is situated in the center of our forehead, in between our eyebrows (between the hypothalamus and pituitary glands). It controls the body. Knowledge of the soul gives the power to realize oneself. The most wonderful attribute of a soul is the ability to record whatever it sees forever. However, the percentage of retrieval power differs from person to person.

The Soul Has Three Faculties

1. **Mind**: Creates thoughts.
2. **Intellect**: Analyzes, filters, visualizes the thoughts created as it needs proof.
3. **Resolve**: Repetitive thoughts formulated into a habit *(Sanskaar)*.

The mind can never be in a "zero-thought" stage. When we create fewer thoughts than our normal range, we feel lighter and happier. Meditation helps us have control over our thoughts and actions. All of us have a soul and its faculty of intellect. Concentration happens when our mind and intellect work in consonance with each other. But the need of the hour is to have a holistic intellect. Such people are givers and will always help others.

What Are the Original Properties of the Soul (PPPLBHK)?

Original properties of the soul are what we all want:

1. **P**eace
2. **P**urity
3. **P**ower
4. **L**ove
5. **B**liss
6. **H**appiness
7. **K**nowledge

When any of the seven properties are depleted in our soul, we keep asking and searching for them outside, in spite of having them all within us, because of the darkness of knowledge within us. Material possessions give us comfort but cannot give us happiness, which lies within.

Karma is the balance sheet of your past and present actions and deeds. Your positive thoughts and virtues are your assets and the vices are your liabilities.

Harmony in any relationship is based on the equibalance of these seven original properties of the soul. These are the properties we ask for in our prayers, too. Through meditation, these seven properties resurge within us, and in doing so the five vices, **A**ttachment, **L**ust, **G**reed, **A**nger, and **E**go **(ALGAE)**, get dissolved.

Who Is the Supreme Soul and Where Does He Reside?

Supreme Soul is *God*, the Divine Power. He is also a point of light, same as the soul. He is an ocean of knowledge, love, peace, patience, and purity. He resides in the soul *(incorporeal)* world, orange-gold in color, which is high up beyond the corporeal world (Earth), the solar system, and the astral/angelic world.

What Is Karma/Karmic Cycle?

Karma is the balance sheet of your past and present actions and deeds. Your positive thoughts and virtues are your assets and the vices are your liabilities. You cannot escape or avoid settling your karmic account. However, you can reduce its impact by indulging in good deeds, serving mankind and being in constant connection with the Supreme Power.

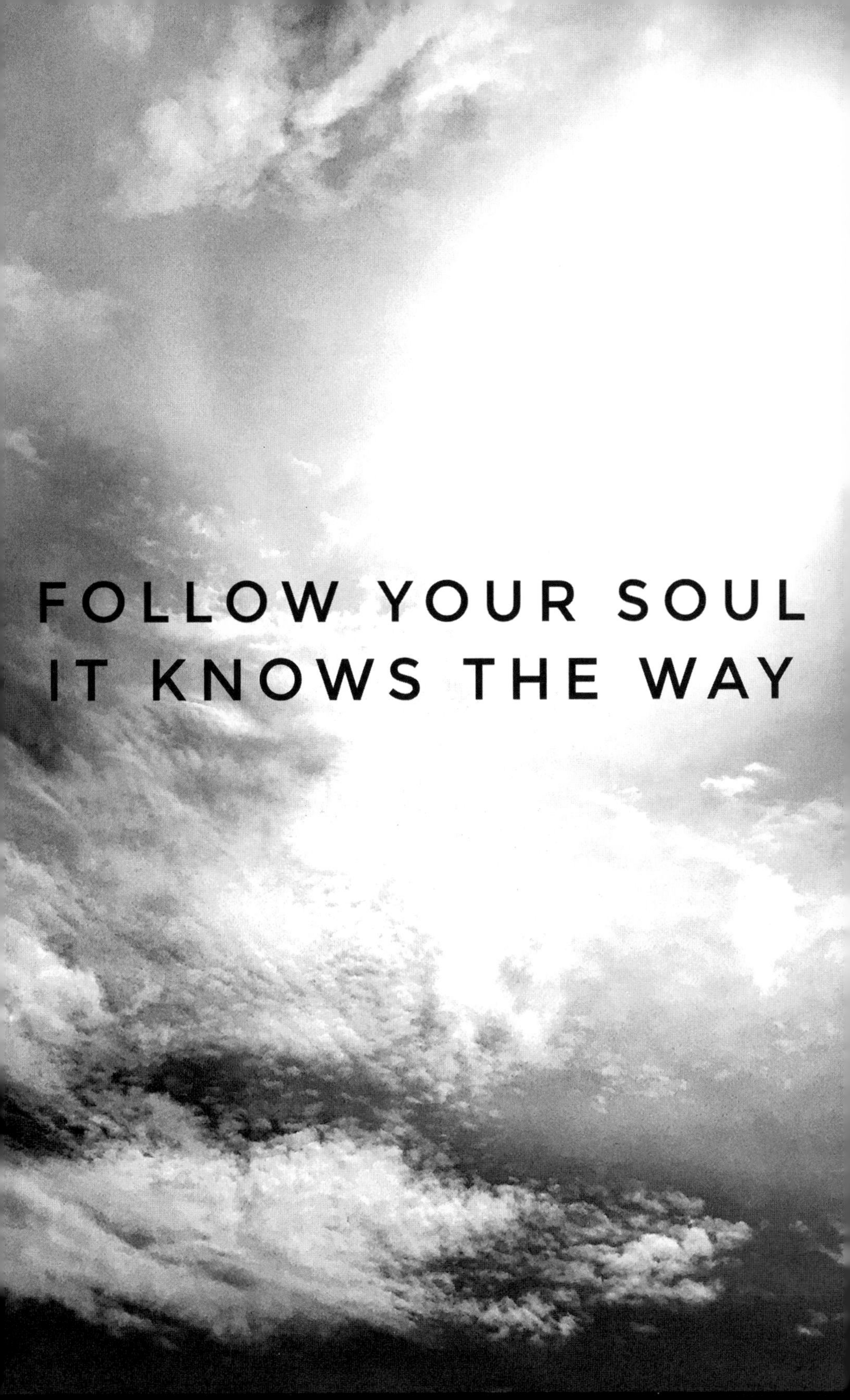
FOLLOW YOUR SOUL
IT KNOWS THE WAY

CHAPTER 1

THE DIVINE CONNECTION

*P*ractice being in a state of soul consciousness with prayers, meditation, and silence. Recharge the battery of your soul to match the frequency of the Supreme Power.

Purity of Soul

Purity is the original state of being of any soul. It is our inherent nature, which gets contaminated when it transcends from the spiritual world to the world of emotions and attachments. An impure soul attracts negativity and drifts away from its connection with the divine. In order to re-establish this connection, you need to be detached from worldly connections and set yourself free from all vices. Keep your thoughts clean, speak good words, and do good deeds. It is the very essence of any religion or way of life. It gets you closer to God.

Positive Virtues Shape the Character and Morale of a Person

The value worth of a person is determined by the positive virtues he/she holds.

Courage, love, kindness, generosity, empathy, and humanity are a few examples of positive virtues that build and strengthen the character of a person and affect his/her behavior and attitude towards life and others. An abundance of positive virtues attributes to good behavior. Good behavior spreads good vibrations. Good vibrations are symbolic of divine presence, and where God exists, life is a blessing!

Silence Is Music in the Storm of Words

Silence is the language of the tranquil mind of an enriched soul. You can hear its voice only when your mind is at peace. It is more powerful than words, and it adds to your inner strength. Conserve your word power and speak only when necessary. Beautiful words by Buddha:

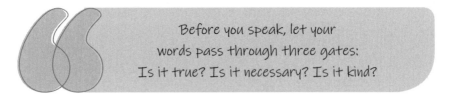

Before you speak, let your words pass through three gates: Is it true? Is it necessary? Is it kind?

Silence is the music of the Supreme Power. Adjust your frequency to stay tuned.

Peace Is Experiencing Silence in Chaos

Peace begins with acceptance of yourself and life as it is. Make a conscious effort to keep your mind away from things that disturb you, and engage in activities that enhance your happiness and help you calm your senses and emotions, like being in the company of good souls and

> Peace first sets within and then emits around.

exchanging good thoughts. Look at every soul with love, and learn to accept their shortcomings. Peace first sets within and then emits around.

Soul Consciousness

Consider yourself to be a soul, not a body. Being in a constant state of the soul's awareness is called *soul consciousness*. It does not come naturally to everybody. It needs to be practiced with a focused mind and

> A soul never dies. It only travels from one body to another in the cycle of birth and death.

guided support. Feeling bodiless itself takes away most of the sufferings and negative feelings from you. It makes you feel lighter, peaceful, and joyous. There is nothing to compare and compete with, so we are all on the same page respecting each other's emotions and sentiments. It eliminates the fear of death, as it brings in the realization that a soul never dies. It only travels from one body to another in the cycle of birth and death. It elevates your state of being and strengthens the bonding with the Supreme Soul, God. *It is a gateway to paradise.*

Prayer: A Soul-to-Soul Communication with God

Prayer is just a conversation with God. *Even a casual hello to God is prayer.* It is the simplest and most effective form of communication with the divine.

> Even a casual hello to God is prayer.

Prayer is the whisper of our soul and yet it is heard the loudest and the clearest by the divine. It is not confined to religion, need or want, and it reaches beyond distance and time. So, make it an integral part of your routine.

Meditation Is Listening to God and Feeling His Presence

With the busy lives we lead, full of commitments and responsibilities, slaves of time, there comes the need to give your thoughts and mind the much-needed break to pause, to relax, to breathe in calmness, and to breathe out stress. We need to silence the traffic of our thoughts and balance the outburst of our emotions. This is possible by bringing some discipline to our regular routine and making time to be with ourselves. Quieten your mind, drive away the many thoughts that race through it and focus your concentration to think nothing. Listen to the voice of stilled silence, which is the voice of God, and feel his presence. This process is called meditation. There are various methods of meditation taught and shared by experts and spiritual gurus in seminars, workshops, social media, audios, videos, books, spiritual organizations, etc. It is the need of the hour to learn these techniques that best suit our convenience and make them a part of our daily routine. Frequency and duration are subjective to a person's priority and time available. The suggested minimum is five to ten minutes per day; gradually increasing it.

As per Brahmakumaris-Raj Yoga meditation, the best time to meditate is in the wee hours of the morning between 2:00 a.m. and 5:00 a.m., called the *Brahma Muhurta,* or *Amritevala*, when God showers his choicest blessing on his children who reach out to Him through meditation. It's important to note that *making time for meditation does not take away time from your busy schedule. In fact, it adds more time to your day. With meditation, your creativity, energy levels, productivity, and pace of work increase.*

Meditation teaches you to enjoy your present moment. It balances your emotions and controls your temperament and increases your patience and acceptance levels. It energizes your being, recharges your soul, and keeps your health in check. With regular practice, it will bring about a significant change in your personality, health, and outlook towards life. You will feel feather light, experience sudden bouts of happiness, and the magical presence of God, which cannot be explained and described but only experienced and cherished. *Meditate, and take charge of your life!*

> Making time for meditation does not take away time from your busy schedule.

SIMPLE EXAMPLE: HOW TO MEDITATE FOR BEGINNERS (MINIMUM FIVE TO TEN MINUTES)

- Prepare your mind that you are going to have an enjoyable experience that will relax your body and soul.
- Sit or lay down in a relaxed position, preferably in a quiet place.
- Close your eyes or keep them open.
- Loosen your body; be relaxed.
- Try to concentrate on your breathing and the overall feel of your body.
- Rajyoga meditation teaches you to practice soul consciousness, to consider yourself to be a soul (a point of light) and connect with the Supreme Soul (the divine point of light) through your imagination and visualization.
- Do not get distracted with the many thoughts that might wander through your mind or the noises you hear in your surroundings. Let them come and go. Do not concentrate on them.
- Slowly, your breathing would become shallow, and you will only hear the sound of your breathing.

- As time passes by, your mind and body will relax.
- You will start feeling lighter.
- If you're awake and you manage to reach the ultimate stage of meditation with regular practice, you will feel your body elevate and rise above the ground; you will feel bodiless, with a magical quietness and calm. You will feel you are in paradise and in close connection with God.
- Enjoy the moment.
- Slowly, come back to observing your breathing. Start becoming aware of your surroundings, and wake up or set an alarm.
- You will be fresh and as energized as a blooming flower.
- There is a possibility that you might go to sleep during meditation due to deep relaxation. It's okay. Go with the flow.
- You can use guided audio or music for meditation if you so desire.
- You can even set up the ambience in your place of meditation by having a dim light on or by lighting an aroma candle that will fill up your senses and set you in a tranquil mood.

Being Humane

When we treat others with kindness, humility and empathy, and look beyond their imperfections, we are being humane. It is an elevated level of thinking that enhances the personality of a person and stands out distinctly from the rest. Impulsive reactions and outbursts of negative emotions like anger, hatred, and disgust and focusing on one's weaknesses and inefficiencies or follies is very easy. What is difficult but appreciable is the ability to keep emotions and tolerance levels in check and to view the other person or situation with humanity to help them sail through the tide. This is the attitude of a humane person whose heart is full of love and compassion, whose every thoughtful gesture and humane reaction is a reflection of the nature of God.

> To err is human, to forgive, divine. All people commit sins and make mistakes. God forgive them, and people are acting in a godlike (divine) way when they forgive.
>
> —Alexander Pope

Share and Care

In today's world of give-and-take, where nothing comes for free, it is difficult to find a heart that bleeds for others' sufferings and for whom touching as many lives as possible, filling their lives with abundance and helping others to hold on to their hope, is prioritized over personal needs and gains. If you come across such people in your life, savor their relationship and consider yourself blessed. Our world needs such people who understand the true essence of life, who befriend others, who fill up the void in our lives, who give us a reason to smile and show us the path of life. Be that torch of light and spread joy.

Service to Mankind

When we reach out to people in distress and need and direct our energy and efforts to helping them, comforting them, and bringing a ray of hope in their lives, we are engaging in a selfless act of love, care, and concern and moving closer towards God. This is what God expects each one of us to do. He wants us to be His extended hands and do the noble work of reaching out to people, lifting up their spirits and spreading the message of love, peace, and happiness.

Leap of Faith: Believe, Feel, and Think

Trying is confidence. Holding back with fear is weakness.

On our spiritual quest, faith plays a vital role. It is important that we have faith in the path we have chosen to travel from where we are to where we want to be. Besides, there must be a willingness to believe that change is inevitable and that whatever happens is for the best. Feel your passions and dreams take shape as you progress in your committed efforts to transform yourself and, in turn, the world to a paradise of happiness and joy. *Think positive, and be optimistic in every walk of life. Wade through the hurdles with faith in every stride.* Step out of your comfort zone and take a chance. *Trying is confidence. Holding back with fear is weakness.*

Angels: Messengers of God

It is believed that God deploys his messengers, or angels, in human form to guide us, to be there for us, and to help us. These guardian angels guide us at the behest of God, hold our hand in the hour of need, and show the support and presence of the Almighty in our lives. These are normal people we meet on our life's path for a reason, and at times for a season. They ride the chariot of our passions and dreams and take us to the desired destination with love and care. They touch our lives in a special way. They are special, they are kind, and they are sent to our lives by God with a motive, a purpose, that rolls out in time and catches us unawares in a pleasant way. Each one of us comes across these messengers in some stage in our life. They play their part and exit or become an inseparable part of our life. *Be a messenger of God and enrich lives!*

Energy Recharge

Every day of our lives, we engage in various mental and physical activities, meet people with different vibrations, get stressed out over pressing responsibilities, commitments, and deadlines at our workplace and home. All of this drains us of our energy at physical and soul levels, reduces our level of enthusiasm, affects our creativity and brings down our productivity. If we continue to carry on with such low energy levels for a long stretch of time without a recharge, it affects our spiritual and physical health adversely. Thus, comes the need to re-energize our discharged soul and empower it on a day-to-day basis, or perhaps at regular intervals during the day, just as we charge our cellphones. This energy recharge of the soul can be done by connecting to the powerhouse of energy, God, at regular intervals during the day by engaging in silence and focusing your thoughts on the Supreme Power, bathing in His light and energy.

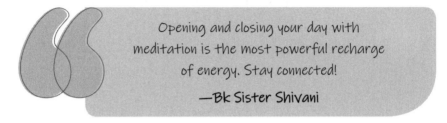

Opening and closing your day with meditation is the most powerful recharge of energy. Stay connected!

—Bk Sister Shivani

Spiritual Progress

When you are a soulful person treading on the path of spirituality, depending upon the intensity of your interest and involvement, you tend to progress gradually.

Lots of significant changes happen within you. You tend to be more conscious of your thoughts, your surroundings, your actions, and reactions, and your attitude towards life and others. You are an edge above all. You may or may not realize it soon. You do not feel normal. You undergo changes in your feelings, and you cannot easily express or explain them to yourself or others. It's a weird but good feeling. There is a sudden calmness in you.

There is a change in your level of tolerance. It feels like your personality is undergoing a sudden makeover and your intellect is set on a different mode. Your personal wishes and desires seem to take a backseat, and your focus shifts from yourself to the well-being of others. You seem to be moved by seeing others in suffering, stronger than ever, and you cannot hold yourself from reaching out to them and helping them get out of the situation. The thought pattern elevates to another level of higher consciousness.

Anger sublimates to love. You tend to empathize with others. You take charge of any situation and change and accommodate yourself to sustain harmony in life and relationships. You forgive and forget easily and work on mending relationships. You dare to dream and work towards making them come true. You are able to balance your emotions and strive to be stable in the most trying circumstances. Incidents occur to teach you a higher lesson as you take a step above. You become vulnerable to vibrations and energies. You speak your mind and keep yourself away from negativity and people who drain you of your energy.

You feel sudden bouts of happiness and surges of excessive energy and anxiety, with a positive feel, that cannot be easily understood or explained but just felt. Gratitude becomes a part of your routine and gets expressed any time and every time, without a conscious effort. You become more of a giver, without any expectations. Life becomes a bunch of surprises, but you enjoy every moment and have the ability to deal with it and have a positive output. It's a beautiful experience. Feel it!

CHAPTER 2

THE JOURNEY
WITHIN

Search your soul. Move out of the shadows of your past and raise your emotional quotient by defining and redefining your purpose in life. Focus on its clear vision.

The journey within begins when we accept and believe that all the answers we look for are right here within us. All we need to do is be introspective.

Search Your Soul: Find the Real You

Do you know who you are and your purpose in life?

> You will find your answers if you ask the right questions.

Explore the real you by spending time with yourself. Look within. Indulge in inner dialogue. Go to the depths of your thoughts and feelings. *You will find your answers if you ask the right questions.* Your wants will be replaced by your real needs, and you will find the path you are meant to tread upon.

Childhood Impressions Are Sensitive and Long-Lasting

Relationships and incidences in our childhood leave long-lasting impressions on our subconscious mind. These impressions tend to surface as our personality traits, habits, fears, and anxieties with the passage of time. At times, we can get lucky if we recognize the past and current connection, acknowledge it and make timely corrections to control the situation. However, if left unnoticed, they can have a significant impact on one's current life.

What You Think You Are…

Thoughts create your destiny. What you thought you attracted, what you will now think you will receive. So, to create a glorious future, you need to think positive thoughts. The frequency emitted by your thoughts and affirmations is what will shape your destiny.

Habits Shape Your Personality

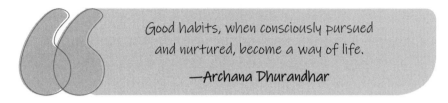

Good habits, when consciously pursued and nurtured, become a way of life.
—Archana Dhurandhar

We need to groom our soul through constant introspection, regular intake of nourishing food, positive influences, good company, and spiritual awakening. Habits shape our personality. They are a reflection of our inner self: Our behavior, reactions, and ideologies.

Realize Your Self-Worth and Rise Above

When you search your soul and find the real you, you need to have a talk with yourself. Look into the mirror, acknowledge yourself, and love and admire the creation of God. Do it as often as you can. It boosts your self-esteem and self-worth and has a positive impact on your personality.

Raise Your Emotional Quotient and Strengthen Relationships

Emotional quotient (EQ) is our emotional intelligence, wherein we are conscious and aware of our own feelings and those of others too. It affects our attitude and behavioral impact on others, on personal and professional fronts. We can raise this emotional quotient by acknowledging and correcting our emotional shortcomings, being empathetic towards others, offering a patient ear, and being open to new ideas and suggestions. This, in turn, establishes peace and harmony in relationships.

Trust Your Instincts: They Are Seldom Wrong

An instinct is a gut feeling that emerges from within. It overrides facts and judgments. It's a strong feeling, an inner voice we often tend to ignore. It is believed that our instincts are seldom wrong, as they could be messages from our soul guides. We need to trust and follow them.

False Beliefs Influence Our Thoughts and Feelings: Correct Them in Time!

We are often misled and misguided by our own false beliefs and preconceived notions.

They affect our attitude and power of judgment. Change your thought pattern. Give the other person the benefit of the doubt. Do not be biased or prejudiced. Observe the impacts of your beliefs on you and others.

Find the Real Purpose of Your Life: Redefine It and Work Towards It

As we progress in our spiritual journey and attain the stage of soul consciousness, we are able to hear our inner calling. There is a sudden surge of energy within us that gives us an insight into who we are, what we are meant to do, and where we need to go. Once we acknowledge and accept it, our real journey begins. From that point on, our life changes. All our efforts and energies are directed towards defining and redefining its real purpose.

Trust Your Wings and Fly

We come across different kinds of people. Some dare to dream and go get it! Some cage their dreams within themselves, due to fear of acknowledgment, low self-esteem, probable outcome, or others' reactions. By caging our dreams, we are holding back our emotions. This adversely affects our thoughts and behavior; there is a feeling of constant anxiety dwelling within us that needs to be released. Sharing a beautiful thought penned down by an unknown writer:

> A bird sitting on a tree is never afraid of a branch breaking, because its trust is not on the branch, but on its own wings.

Be an Enlightened Soul

Live in your present. Establish a spiritual connection with the divine. Invest your time in being a compassionate human being. *Stir your soul with meditation and prayers.* Follow your inner calling.

Stir your soul with meditation and prayers.

Be the epitome of love, peace, and strength. Be light and spread light. Be the enlightened one. Use the law of attraction to make things happen your way. Let the universe conspire to fulfill your innermost desires.

Let go of
BLAME

Let go of
ANGER

Let go of
REGRET

Let go of
FEAR

CHAPTER 3

LET-GO ATTITUDE

*D*elete "was" and control "is"; travel light. Shift your thoughts, change your regular way of thinking with a new perspective; cleanse your soul and conserve energy.

De-clutter Wasteful Thoughts

Just as we often de-clutter our home and remove all that is not needed, we need to empty the garbage of wasteful thoughts from our mind from time to time, too. Removal of unwanted thoughts releases the unnecessary burden and influence of negativity on our feelings, actions, and deeds and creates room for positive thoughts.

Control Your Thoughts and Be Stable

Take charge of your thoughts; do not let them control you.

> Take charge of your thoughts; do not let them control you.

Attain stability by responding rather than reacting to a situation. Choose your thoughts wisely, as they will determine your future. A silent and tranquil mind will regulate the thought process and optimize stability.

Bury Your Past: Lay the Foundation Today and Build Your Future

Leave your past behind. Consider it a full stop, with no strings attached. Utilize its teachings and experience to lay down the foundation for your today and the glorious future ahead. Your today is a result of your yesterday, and your tomorrow depends on how well you invest in your today.

Delete "Was" and Control "Is"

There is no point pondering over what we had and what could be. We cannot undo our past, so it's wise to just delete "was" from our system and lives.

Today you are the master of your mind; you are in charge of what you have. You can move the world with your thoughts, so focus your concentrated efforts on your present and control your "is".

Drop the Negatives and Hold the Positives

Throughout our life journey, we come across various circumstances, good and bad, that help us gain experiences to deal with life and its offerings. All experiences are not welcome; neither can they be completely erased from our memories. But it's prudent for us to look at the positive side of every situation, and flip the negative to our advantage and move on. As we progress and look back, we tend to realize that the negatives also added essential hue to the fabric of our life. They were an integral part of a supreme plan to either teach you a lesson or grant you a worthy experience.

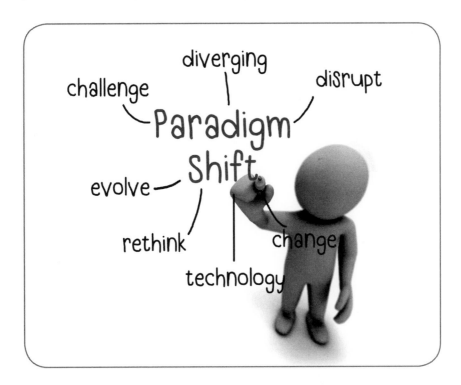

Curbed Desires Lead to Emotional Blockages: Release Them!

Unacknowledged and unfulfilled wishes and desires leave a void within you. Suppressed feelings are negative emotions and lead to emotional blockages that affect your physical and emotional well-being. There has to be a closure to everything. Scan your thoughts, and release these negative emotions.

Seal the Emotional Drains

We can change our moods by choosing and replacing one thought over another.

Often our attachments to people, places, and things keep us hooked to expectations. And when unfulfilled, these expectations lead to disappointments and resentment. These lead to emotional drains. In such circumstances, we need to uplift our dampened spirits, replace our thoughts of scarcity with abundance, step out from the shadows of the past and seal the emotional drains.

Shift Your Thought, Change Your Life

Our thoughts affect our feelings, and our feelings affect our actions and ultimately our outlook towards life. We need to realize the power of our thoughts. We can change our moods by choosing and replacing one thought over another. With this shift of thought, we can change how we feel about and react to a given situation. This helps us be in harmony with situations and relationships at all times.

Change Your Paradigm: Get a New Life Purpose

A change of paradigm is a gradual shift of perspective, or a way of looking at things differently. When we let go of our primitive thought patterns, rigid viewpoints, and preconceived notions or perceptions, the outcome will open newer avenues to explore and tread upon. Dare to think differently; open the secret doors to success and happiness.

Tune in to Your Vibrations

To enhance our energy levels, we need to set the frequency of our vibrations to the frequency of the divine power. Besides meditation, silence, and divine connection, vibrations can also be purified by surrounding yourself with people who uplift you and help you rise in life. The company you keep influences your thoughts and reactions. The higher the vibrational energy, the higher the level of soul consciousness and purity. The lower the vibrational energy, the higher the vulnerability for attracting negativity.

Cleanse Your Soul and Attain Spiritual Progress

Remove the toxins of negativity that have contaminated the soul over time with your very own past and present karmic accounts, which need to be settled in this lifetime. However, do not engage in the blame game, and do not ask, "Why me?" *Live your karma graciously. Deal with it and move on.* Tread on the path of spiritual progress.

Connect and Reconnect with the Divine to Energize Your Being

Just as we need to recharge our cell phone battery with its charger, our energy gets depleted by the toxic influences of our own negative and wasteful thoughts, or by the people we interact with or our emotional drains. To replenish our energy, we need to connect and reconnect to the powerhouse of energy—God, through the medium best suited to you, be it a prayer, visualization, listening to or chanting mantras, or just Om.

Forgive and Forget

Let go of feelings of hatred and revenge. *Forgiveness is an act of kindness and a positive emotion for both the forgiver and the forgiven.* Forget what holds you back and makes you feel unhappy. Life is too short to live with anger and hatred. Exchange love for hate. When we forgive and forget, we actually help ourselves stay calm, able to savor relationships and situations.

Travel Light

Let go of not only your past baggage of hurt, disappointments, failures, grudges, and resentments but most importantly your *ego! It's is the "I" that holds you back from traveling light.*

Move On: Life Goes On

> It's is the "I" that holds you back from traveling light.

Nothing lasts forever. We cannot hold on to our past and its misgivings. We have to emerge as fighters, not losers. We need to set our life on play mode and be a silent spectator, totally detached and untouched, and let the story unfold.

ACCEPT WHAT IS,
LET GO OF WHAT WAS,
AND HAVE FAITH IN
WHAT WILL BE.

What you think,
you become.
What you imagine,
you create.

:·)

CHAPTER 4

THOUGHT CREATES DESTINY

*B*elieve in the power of thought. What you think—so it is. Analyze and
filter the quality of your thoughts and feelings. Master the art of
visualization, and welcome destiny.

Quality Analysis of Thoughts Should Be an Automated and Continual Process

We need to train our mind to be in a constant state of consciousness,
aware of the kinds of thoughts that race through our mind and the internal
and external factors influencing them. We need to listen to the voice of
our subconscious mind, which always tells us what is correct and what is
wrong, and take charge of our thoughts. Once we discipline our thought
flow, thought quality will improve while thought quantity is reduced, and
peace will prevail.

Filter Your Thoughts with the Funnel of Purity

Once we start analyzing the quality of our thoughts, we can filter them to keep the positives and drop the negatives. With the power of mind and purity of soul, negative thoughts can be replenished with positives ones. Filtering thoughts regularly will help cleanse and sanitize our thoughts.

Thoughts and Feelings Go Hand in Hand

If we want to feel happy, we need to create happy thoughts, no matter the situation. Our thoughts directly reflect upon our feelings, and, in turn, our feelings dictate our thoughts. We need to strike a balance.

Positive Thinking Is the Password to Success

Positive thoughts keep us in a positive frame of mind and yield positive outputs. When we think good thoughts, we feel good and perform optimally. Positive thoughts add clarity and focus to all our endeavors. Success is then a given.

Power of Intention Magnifies Output

When we apply a powerful intention to a given thought, our entire focus and energies are concentrated on this thought, which escalates its journey from seed to plant.

Reiki teaches us how to add the power of intent to our thoughts to invoke the universal energy. However, we need to observe the ethics of spirituality and use this power of intent only for a good cause.

A Healthy Diet of Thoughts Is Essential for Our Well-Being

Just as we are cautious of wear and tear on our physical health, we need to take care of our mental and spiritual health, too. We need to slow down our flow of thoughts and engage in silence at frequent intervals during the day to de-stress, rejuvenate, and re-energize. Optimizing the quality of thoughts will enhance mental and physical well-being.

> When the lens is hazy, the vision is a blur. When the lens is clear, reality is near.

Adjust Your Thought Focus to Click Your Dream Picture

Prioritize your dreams. Adjust your focus, and concentrate your power of intent and universal energy to a chosen priority. Click and capture the moment to bring your dream to life.

Thought Clarity Is a Step Closer to Reality

When we create a thought about a need, a desire, or a want with a clear intention that is devoid of ambiguity, the accuracy of output is enhanced. When our thoughts are clear, our vision is clear, and we visualize and feel what we believe. *When the lens is hazy, the vision is a blur. When the lens is clear, reality is near.*

Pause! Discipline and Regulate the Flow of Thoughts

With the thousands of thoughts racing through our mind comes the need to discipline and regulate the flow of our thoughts. We need to pause for a minute, preferably every hour or during transition periods, by simply spending time alone in silence. To recharge and restart, drink a glass of water to cool your body and senses and give your thoughts a much-needed break. This can even be practiced at your workplace to keep you focused throughout the day.

Vibration Is an Energy Frequency We Emit into the Universe

Vibrations have a profound impact on people and surroundings. This is the reason why we feel positive vibes in holy places or when we meet good people. We can improve and change the energy of our vibration by realigning our frequency to the frequency of the divine through soul consciousness, purifying our mind, body, and soul, and having positive thoughts and feelings.

Visualize: Bring Your Thoughts to Life, Ahead of Time

Along with a positive intent, if we visualize what we want, we actually add enormous power and energy to thoughts with the belief they will happen. When we visualize with clear intent and feel the emotion ahead of time, we craft our future. Our thoughts sketch our needs, desires, and wants. Add the color of intent to it and the visualization becomes a trailer of our movie in the making.

You Reap What You Sow

We have the power to create, replace, delete, and energize our thoughts.

If we savor good food for thought, we nourish our thoughts and reap positive impacts on our feelings and well-being. Planting the seeds of good thoughts is not enough. They need to be nurtured with values and positive attributes. *The weeds of negativity need to be plucked as and when required to ensure the garden of our mind is in eternal bloom.*

Thought Travels Beyond Space and Time

With the power of intent and spiritual frequency, thoughts can travel beyond space and time. Like any form of travel, we need to decide the itinerary and plan our journey of thought to reach the destination of our choice by arranging our thoughts in the desired sequence and at the appropriate frequency.

> Let the party begin. Occasions to celebrate will follow.

Attract What You Want in Life by Visualizing It, Acknowledging It with Gratitude, and Celebrating the Moment Even Before It Happens; So Will It Be

Visualizations bring you closer to your dream. Acknowledging with gratitude adds to blessings, and celebrating ahead of time seals the moment as an upcoming reality. *Let the party begin. Occasions to celebrate will follow.*

Craft Your Thoughts Carefully, and Welcome Your Destiny

Channel your thoughts to what you want to do and where you want to be. Destiny does not roll out on its own. We create our own destiny through the thoughts we chose to create and harvest. You have the power to bring on the destiny of your choice, because you are the sculptor of your dreams.

TIME MANAGEMENT

RELAX WITH HOBBY

MEDITATE

KEEP CALM & BOOST HAPPINESS

MENTAL HEALTH TIPS
TO REDUCE STRESS

POSITIVE THINKING

TRAVEL

LAUGH

EXCERCISE

MUSIC THERAPY

CHAPTER 5

FOOD FOR THOUGHT

*J*ust as your body requires a balanced diet of nutrients to remain healthy, your thoughts must also be fed with values in the form of good reads, music, mantras, and inspirational quotes, especially when you rise with the sunshine and retire under the blanket of stars.

Emotional Health

Body and health consciousness is the New Age mantra. People binge on diet foods and are attracted towards naturopathy. However, emotional health has not yet caught the spotlight as an important element of our overall well-being.

It is imperative that we realize how important taking care of the health of our mind is. Our emotional health is determined by the quality of thoughts we create every moment of our life. Thoughts have a direct correlation with our feelings, physical health, attitude, relationships, moral ethics, and the energy we emit to the environment. *Our thoughts are the catalyst for emotional health.*

Factors Influencing Our Thoughts

> **Our thoughts are the catalyst for emotional health.**

It is difficult to list all the factors that influence our thoughts. However, we can broadly categorize them as our impressions of the past, the information we seek from what we see, hear and read, and the perceptions acquired through the journey of life.

As souls, we have the capacity to discipline the quantity and quality of the thoughts we create by making a disciplined, conscious effort to offset the factors influencing them that are detrimental to our interests. These were detailed in the previous chapters. We also need to channel and empower our thoughts to increase the frequency levels of positive vibrations in and around us.

Empty Your Mind for a Refill of Energy, Positivity, and Abundance Today and Every Day

Excessive food intake leads to indigestion. If you continue filling a glass beyond its capacity, it will spill over. Stagnant water becomes contaminated over time with the air pollutants and negative energy it breathes. This contaminated water needs to be emptied and refilled with pure fresh water.

The same applies to our thoughts and mind. A daily refill of positive energy is possible when we create the required empty space daily by recycling our thoughts.

Vitamin E (Energy)

Be careful of your daily intake of information. Observe its effect on your feelings, moods, and well-being. If whatever activity you are engaged in makes you feel lighter, happier, and recharged, it resonates with positivity. Similarly, if your spirits are dampened, and you feel heavy and low, it relates to negativity. Positive or negative feelings are the result of the energy field created around us and the vibrations emitted by our own words, actions, and deeds. These are initiated by the thoughts we choose to create on a given day, at a given time, by the information we feed our intellect with. Thus, it's important for us to pop a vitamin E (positive energy) every morning and night to keep our awake and sleep hours energized and harmonized.

From where and how will you get this vitamin E? You receive this positive energy from the cosmos. It has an abundance of positive energy. Channel your thoughts to connect to this source of energy, and draw it into your intellect with powerful intent; feel its vibrations empower your soul and your entire well-being. The moment you feel it, you have it. This positive energy will work like water, an elixir of life, for your thoughts. Consuming it at the opening and closing hours of your day will keep you hydrated with fresh and pure thoughts.

Sanitize Your Thoughts

Just as you sow the appropriate seed to grow the plant you desire, it is important to keep sowing the right seeds of value and knowledge to grow the plant of wisdom. The seeds need to be nurtured by watering them daily with pure content in the form of information intake. When we do something on a repetitive basis, it gradually becomes our *Sanskar,* or habit. Hence, *it's important to have "thought sanitizers" handy to safeguard us from the dust of negativity.* Pick the thought sanitizer of your choice that best cleans your intellect; there are plenty available in the market and on social media in the form of music, mantras, books, videos, spiritual discourses, etc.

Regularity and Discipline Aid Fitness

If we wish to enjoy emotional health on a long-term basis, we need to work out at the mind gym on a daily basis, at fixed time intervals if possible, so that it becomes an integral part of our routine and comes effortlessly to us. Many enthusiastic fitness lovers who want to get their body in shape do rigorous workouts at gyms, spending long hours and lots of money. Dedicated and committed regular efforts result in wonders and change the complete outlook of a person. However, it does not last forever. The moment you stop practicing, you begin to lose it. Working out in a mind gym is comparatively inexpensive, as it is you who creates the thoughts, and it is you who can change them. It's all in your control. The available resources at our disposal only guide us towards how to work on our thoughts. Here again, persistent and consistent efforts made willingly stir our thoughts to radiate positive energy, but they must be continual in nature for a lasting effect that keeps your soul charged.

Stop and Check

When you are not maintaining good health, your body has a way of signaling you to stop and check in. Most of the time, we ignore the signals and carry on with our routine as if nothing has happened, until a point is reached when we have no choice but to stop, seek appropriate medication, and heal. We do not attempt to discover the root causes as we do not have the time, nor do we feel the need. We choose to seal the drains only when diseases manifest. *Just as with the body, our feelings also give us cues to stop and check.* What is it that is bothering us? How deep is the wound? What triggered it? What can we do to heal it? We know all the answers, but it's all a blur, as our intellect is fogged by our lifestyle and thinking pattern. We have no time to turn inwards. We react without thinking; obviously, the outcome is not rewarding. If we train our minds to stop at regular intervals and let our thoughts pass through the quality check, we will be able to take control of our thoughts and heal ourselves better.

> It's important to have "thought sanitizers" handy to safeguard us from the dust of negativity.

Separate the Herbs from the Weeds

Every source of information; be it through social media, television, newspapers, the Internet and so on, offers a mix of healthy and unhealthy ingredients. It's for us to choose those that nourish our thoughts with ease and convenience. We live in the instant age. The quick fix is a mantra we follow, not by choice but by the need of the hour. Time management and quality control have gained prominence. Utmost care needs to be taken to ensure that we do not become trapped in the sticky web of temptations that are sources of entertainment that deplete us of our energy and virtues.

Garnish with Silence

With the variety and flavors of prepared food for thought available in the market, it's more important than ever to garnish every meal of thought with silence. Just as we have tastemakers (positive affirmations, spiritual talks/videos, music for relaxation of body and soul...) to flavor our thoughts and add some thrill, we need taste breakers such as *silence* to pause the speed of wandering thoughts and allow them to flow in rhythm.

Fix a Diet Plan or Menu

A balanced diet of pure and positive thoughts needs to be meticulously followed to ensure optimal mental and emotional health.

Just as a trip is best executed with a planned itinerary, mental fitness can best be maintained by designing a well-balanced menu, including dos and don'ts, best suited to every individual's tastes and preferences, and an inner urge to pursue the same. It needs to be executed with free will and intention, with no force whatsoever. When you relish what you eat, it keeps you happy and healthy. Consuming anything that includes discontentment and resentment disturbs your energy levels, which in turn affects your well-being.

Vedic Literature and Holy Scriptures Are Our White Blood Cells

Ancient scriptures and literature like the Bhagavadgita and the Holy Bible are sacred and divine food for thought that have been passed on to us by enlightened souls to be a part and parcel of our life's journey. They serve as a lighthouse and guiding stars to illuminate the paths we tread with knowledge and wisdom from the deities and messengers of God.

They empower us with the laws of the universe and karma and introduce us to the Creator of the universe to help us identify our purpose in life. This knowledge plays the role of white blood cells in our body, which fight disease. Absorbing such knowledge regularly helps us eradicate the vices that afflict our mind and help maintain healthy and balanced mind, body, and intellect.

> Soothing music with or without words has the power to uplift our mood and spirit.

Music Sets Up the Rhythm of Life

Soothing music with or without words has the power to uplift our mood and spirit. It has the capacity to charge and heal our mind, body, and soul. Music calms our senses and releases stress. Its beats and waves can work as natural tranquilizers to soothe our body into rest and deep sleep. It slows down the pace of our thoughts and enlivens our moods. It's a stimulator. It sets up our life to dance to the tunes of symphony and harmony. So, indulge in music wholeheartedly, whenever you can, and let it rejuvenate your body and soul while you sit back and relax.

Healer's Galaxy: A Whiff of Fresh Air

All around the globe, there are many individual, organizational and spiritual leaders, and motivational speakers who conduct seminars, workshops, and conversations to spread awareness about the significance of the art of living, the laws of attraction, thought power, soul consciousness, etc., who are healers bringing knowledge, study, practice, and spiritual inclination. They work on our thoughts, belief systems, and willingness to change. This gives us another option to explore ourselves, tap our weaknesses, strengthen them, heal ourselves, and heal the world.

Positive Affirmations

These are auto-suggestions, positive thoughts of empowerment and affirmations that we say to ourselves daily, aloud or within. When repeated, these become a part of our regular routine, which helps manifest them into reality. They need to be spoken with confidence and sure intention, without ambiguity or doubt. You may create your own affirmations for things, people, or situations you would love to have in your life. Repeat them for a given period of time. Feel them, visualize them as having happened, make them happen, and then move on to make many more affirmations to make all your dreams come true. An ideal time to say to them is when you wake up fresh in the morning. Let them be the first thought you create; at night before you sleep, let them be the last thought you create.

EXAMPLES OF POSITIVE AFFIRMATIONS

- I love to spread love, and love comes easily to me.

- I will make my dream come true, and so it is.

- I am at ease with myself in any given situation and have the power to heal.

My day
begins
and ends
with
gratitude

CHAPTER 6

ATTITUDE OF GRATITUDE

*T*hank you is not just an acknowledgment; it's a *blessing*, an act of *divinity* that has a ripple effect.

Acknowledgment Is an Integral Part of Expressing Gratitude

Gratitude is the feeling of being thankful and grateful, a beautiful gesture of reciprocation. It is an elevated thought of thankfulness. **Feeling grateful and not acknowledging it is like dedicating a song to someone and only hearing it yourself.**

Attitude of Gratitude: A Positive Emotion

Gratitude makes you feel happy and lifts your spirits. Positive emotions keep you peaceful and healthy. Cultivate the daily habit of expressing gratitude for the smallest things in life, every time and any time, and experience its magical effects on your well-being. It works!

Expressing Gratitude Is Good Etiquette on Personal and Professional Fronts

The mere act of being thankful and expressing it spontaneously, without any effort, is considered good etiquette. It reflects a positive personality trait and a healthy upbringing. It's an integral part of effective business communication and personal relationships.

Attitude of Gratitude: An Act of Divinity

Gratitude is an act of kindness. When we feel grateful in any situation, we are, in a way, thanking the Almighty. Every thoughtful gesture that touches a soul and attracts blessings is like a prayer to God and thus an act of divinity.

Attitude of Gratitude: An Energy Exchange

How often do we express gratitude to the universe for the blessings it bestows upon us in the form of air, sunlight, water, food, and shelter, which are the basic essentials of life? The truth is, we get so busy looking for the big things in life that these basic essentials go unnoticed, as we tend to take them for granted. However, when we do express gratitude for them, we actually exchange our good, positive energy for universal life force energy.

Attitude of Gratitude: Attracts Abundance

When we are constantly conscious of being grateful and express gratitude with every breath we take, we feel content with whatever we have. This feeling of contentment attracts abundance as a blessing. Write on a piece of paper, *I am in abundance*, feel grateful, and look at it daily with powerful intent. Abundance will follow.

> When we express gratitude, we are on a higher frequency of thought.

An Attitude of Gratitude Enhances Emotional Well-Being

The expression of gratitude is an exchange of a good feeling of acknowledgment. Be grateful before it's too late. There is no point in showering mental *thank you*s after a person is no more. Do it while they can hear you and feel good about themselves. *When we express gratitude, we are on a higher frequency of thought*. Thus, we attract positive emotions of peace, love, and harmony in our lives and enhance our emotional well-being.

Attitude of Gratitude: Build Relationships

A simple *thank you* can move a person and transform negative feelings to positive. Expressing gratitude is an exchange of positive emotions. It makes one feel acknowledged, appreciated, and noticed for a thought, gesture, act, or deed. It establishes a connection and builds and heals relationships.

Attitude of Gratitude:
Optimum Return on Investment

Just a moment of thought that effortlessly expresses a feeling of thankfulness will attract more and more positivity in our life. As per the law of attraction, when you give more, you get more. Thus, when you express good thoughts, goodness is attracted into your life. *Wherever there is goodness, God exists.* He manifests our blessings and optimizes abundance into our lives.

An Attitude of Gratitude Adds to Your Credibility

Wherever there is goodness, God exists.

An attitude of gratitude is a very small gesture, but it exhibits a positive side of your personality. We look up to those people who have the thoughtfulness and presence of mind to express such positive feelings spontaneously and genuinely. It adds to your self-worth and builds up your credible image.

Attitude of Gratitude:
One of the Five Principles of Reiki

An attitude of gratitude is a positive affirmation adopted by Reiki practitioners while healing others with Reiki. It elevates your spiritual energy. It keeps you blessed and in abundance at all times. It helps to keep our ego at bay and enhances the effect of our healing touch.

Thank You: A Blessing

When we express gratitude, we touch people's lives. When the same emotion is returned to us, it becomes a blessing. This is because God teaches us to value small things in life and be happy with what we have. Living with the thought of contentment keeps us happy. Gratitude has the power to change our thoughts and our lives. All we need to do is practice this attitude of gratitude daily and religiously and keep counting our blessings.

Attitude of Gratitude Has a Ripple Effect

When you do something good for someone without any expectation, thoughtfully, someday, it comes back to you and catches you unawares in a pleasant way. This is called a ripple effect. What goes around comes around. Get into the practice of being thankful to more and more people and for more and more things in life. Every day the count should increase. You will be surprised to discover that we have many people and many things in our life to be thankful for. When we start expressing gratitude, we see how well we spend our days with positive emotions and the number of blessings we attract to enrich our lives. One small change will change your life.

Attitude of Gratitude: Make It a Routine

Daily practice of an attitude of gratitude will enrich your life with happiness and joy.

Start and end your day with a *thank you* to God, the universe, nature and your parents, and see positive vibes resonate back at you all day long. Be thankful not only for the positives but the negatives in your life. They are equally essential to make you understand the value of appreciating and being thankful for the smallest things in life.

CHAPTER 7

SPIRIT OF LOVE

*B*e an avatar of love—the most powerful energy in the universe—a
confidante, an anchor to help the needy, to lift one's spirits with an
umbrella of blessings.

Count Your Blessings with Love

Love is a vibration. It is the most beautiful emotion God has gifted to us. It
is a frequency that travels beyond space and time and manifests itself in
the form of positive energy that can elevate a person to the highest level
of happiness. Make love an integral part of your life by loving yourself
first. A glass of water can spill only when its full. Similarly, you have to be
filled to the brim with love in order to give it to others. Love yourself for
what you are and accept yourself unconditionally. Imbibe love with every
thought, action and deed, and feel its magic spread fragrance into our
lives and all around us in the form of showers of blessings.

Love: The Extended Hands of the Almighty

Be the extended hands of the Supreme Power above and reach out to those in need.

Love has the power to re-instill lost faith. It offers the surge of energy to bring back hope and the drive to strive. It adds to your strength and crumbles your weakness.

Be an Emotional Anchor of Love That Holds One in Place

Most of us tend to seek a support system to keep sailing through the journey of life. We find that we need someone to whom we can always reach out without any inhibitions to share and express. Feedback is not a necessity. Just the thought of having someone who can hold you in place, balance your emotions, encourage you to pursue your passion and your dreams, makes a significant impact on one's life and well-being. Your family, your inner circle, and the Almighty are examples of the same. *Be a life jacket of love for someone that may or may not be used but still instills a feeling of safety and security in one's life by its mere existence.*

> Every drop of love you share will condense back into the ocean in time.

Be an Ocean of Infinite Love

It hurts when you missed out on being loved, and it's even more painful when you have love to give but nobody to receive it. Do not limit love with expectations; express it selflessly in abundance. Love is an infinite ocean that can never be empty. Embrace its waves in all the tides of life. *Every drop of love you share will condense back into the ocean in time.*

Patience with Others Is Love

Where love exists, anger dissolves and patience evolves. Patience is keeping a good attitude while waiting. How often do we agree with others' opinions, actions, thoughts, and beliefs? But, when it comes to our loved ones, we tend to adjust and accommodate the order of our thoughts and expectations. This shows how love plays a key role in tuning our behavior and attitude to maintain harmony in relationships and value time.

Love: The Pillar of Strength

You can add to the strength of others only when you overcome your own weaknesses and are strong yourself. *The Almighty God is the powerhouse of love. He is our pillar of strength in every hour of need.* He has bestowed each one of us with the capacity to love in abundance, without limitations. We tend to suppress it beneath shadows of ego, hatred, judgment, criticism, and misunderstanding, which overpower our true potential. To rise above these layers and to emanate love, one has to be in constant connection with the divine.

> Where love exists, anger dissolves and patience evolves.

Don't just be a shoulder to lean on; instead, be a pillar of strength that lifts one's spirits and level of confidence to rise and shine even after the darkest of storms.

Confidante: A Trusted, Loved, and Faithful Being

Most of us share our day-to-day highs and lows with our family and friends. It's a process of offloading information, thoughts, feelings, emotions, achievements, and failures that mount within us to make us feel lighter. However, there are still some thoughts, feelings, and secrets that we feel comfortable to share with only a select few, who have an edge over the rest in terms of trust, faith, and confidence, which are strong attributes of love. This special someone is a confidante who comes in our life as a Samaritan of God and love—a blessing. *Be a Samaritan of love, and touch as many lives as you can.*

Empathy Is Love

An empathetic person is one who has the ability to sense and feel the emotions and feelings of others by placing one's self in another person's shoes. An empathetic person's heart bleeds and feels the pain of seeing people in despair, and his or her actions and reactions work towards healing the situation and the emotions. In itself, this is a selfless act of love and empathy. If more and more people develop an empathetic attitude towards others, life will be full of love and respect, and peace will prevail.

> Be a Samaritan of love, and touch as many lives you can.

Where There Is Love There Is Kindness and Warmth

Kindness is an expression and essence of love. *You cannot remove love from a kindhearted person or kindness from a heart full of love. Where love dwells, kindness blooms.* We need to develop the habit of being kind to ourselves and looking at every person and every situation with a loving heart and a kind attitude. This will shift our perspective and bring happiness into the lives of others and, in turn, ours. *The litmus test of kindness and love is the emotional warmth of goodness we feel within us as we send the same to others.*

Gift of Love

Love is the most precious unconditional gift you can give anyone. Love is not confined to defined relationships. It's an ensemble of expressed feelings, emotions, and virtues. When you fill someone's life with love, you make the other person feel wanted, loved, and cared for. It adds to one's self-worth. It energizes your soul and makes you feel good. And when you feel good, you think good, and your thoughts, actions, and deeds are good. *Real love is to love without expectations.*

Love Makes You Create Time

When you love and care for someone, you never run out of time. Being busy is an excuse, an escape route used for those who do not hold importance or priority in their lives. Again, where there is love there is understanding, and where there is understanding there is respect for each other's time. However, when your heart is full of love and empathy for others, you tend to rearrange your priorities to make time and be there for someone in need, adding to their well-being, which, in itself, attracts gratitude and love and enriches your life with blessings.

Just Being There for Someone Is a Thoughtful Gesture of Love

When we are excited to share some good news or just vent our frustrations or are looking for a patient ear to express our sorrow, we reach out to someone to empty our thoughts. That someone could be God, family, friend, mentor, guardian, or maybe even a pet. Just the thought of having someone to whom we can reach out adds to the feeling of having a support system, someone who cares for our well-being and has the time and patience to hear us out, give us a pat on our back, a warm hug of love or just kind words of encouragement to keep us going. It may not always be possible for us to be a punching bag or a personal diary for someone, but the least we can do is try.

Befriending others and being there for them may not bring us monetary or tangible returns, but the happiness, solace, and smile that we can bring into someone's life will attract inner peace and joy for having been of help to someone, making a small effort towards serving mankind. Also, if we consider the Almighty as our friend, guardian, and mentor, we will never feel lonely or need to look for support in others. God is always there for us. All we need to do is reach out to Him, believe in Him, and know that He will give us only what is best and meant for us, which may not be what we want.

Be an Avatar of Love

Being an avatar of love is the highest level that one can attain as a human, to resonate with love and spread its magic in the league of time. Each one of us has the capacity to attain this level, so far as we believe in ourselves and have a focused intention to work in a committed manner towards making this happen. However, taking a step in this direction is, in itself, a big leap of faith and an inner calling to be part of the big plan of the One above to spread the message of love and restore peace.

Love: The Powerhouse of Energy

Every act and deed enacted with the spirit of love is backed up with a surge of energy from within us, which has a cascading, positive effect on the resulting outcome. This applies to both professional and personal relationships. It's a proven fact that when we love what we do, our motivation and commitment levels are high, and we are never stressed.

We are self-motivated and perform optimally. This also harmonizes our relationships with co-workers, as we always possess an abundance of the positive energy of love. Similarly, in our personal relationships, love also plays an important role in our well-being and state of mind. Harmony in relationships has a direct correlation with our mindset, behavior, and attitude towards others and life. Love keeps us bonded. We care for and respect each other's emotions, and in this way, we keep each other happy. Happiness automatically translates to our well-being.

Love Connects Souls

Sometimes, we coincidentally come across people in life with whom we feel an instant connection, a bonding, as if we have known each other for many lifetimes. It's a strange feeling that cannot be explained but only felt; the heart feels the love, and the soul feels the connection. Most often, these are relationships or friendships that were meant to be, and *the universe orchestrated events to bring these people into our life.*

It's a divine connection, a sacred and pure bonding, where two or more lives have come together to complement and help each other pursue their purposes in life. It could also be a past life connection that has brought them together to complete an unfulfilled task or karma from past lifetimes. *In spirituality, there is no coincidence. It's part of a drama that unveils in time.*

CHAPTER 8

MAGIC OF THE UNIVERSE

P ost a letter of clear thought to the universe, your genie, and unravel its mysteries. Learn the secrets to experience the magic of infinite and unlimited possibilities to celebrate life.

Post a Letter of Clear Thought to the Universe

Everything that exists has energy. There is someone who holds the reins of creation and existence. The universe is the energy field that transcribes every message it receives and echoes back a response. When we say what we think, so it is. It is our thought that travels beyond space and time into this invisible energy and gets its form. Thus, we need to be specific and clear about what we want and create a clear thought, devoid of ambiguity, to transmit into the universe. Clarity of thought relays the exact message, which in turn wins us the desired response.

Clear Signals, Clear Drive-Through

When our conscious mind has a thought, our inner voice, or our subconscious mind, speaks to us, cautions us, guides us, and alerts us about the quality and intent of our thought. However, the intensity and power of the subconscious mind and our ability to hear its voice depend on how active or passive our subconscious mind is. When we are in charge of our thoughts and our reactions to given situations, as detailed in the previous chapters, our awareness levels are enhanced.

> A happy mind charges faster and connects better.

We are more receptive towards these signals, and we come across clearer pathways to drive our thoughts through the universe. Also, we need to have clear communication with the universe. Be specific about what you think you want. If you give mixed signals, the universe will be confused, and you will not get what you want.

Charge to Connect

Just as every electronic gadget needs to be plugged into a charger to energize and function, our soul also needs to be charged at frequent intervals to attain the required energy levels and be attracted by the magnetic pull of the universal energy. *Positive energy is the fuel of the soul.* We can obtain this positive energy by maintaining a healthy mind, body, and soul: By having a disciplined diet of nourishing food for thoughts, simple and nutritious food for the body, regular exercise for physical health, and meditation for the soul. Spend more time with yourself, and do what makes you happy. *A happy mind charges faster and connects better.* Make time to enjoy the beauty and abundance of nature and be recharged by its life force energy.

Spiritual Frequency Is a Mirror of the Soul

Frequency is the language of the universe. It is a vibrational energy. The quality of vibration directly corresponds to your physical, emotional, and mental health. We need to be in a constant state of awareness of our thoughts, actions, and reactions to raise our vibrational energy. *Positive vibrations make you feel lighter, and negative vibrations make you feel heavier.* Every person has a different frequency level, which resonates with the quality of the soul. People with similar frequency or vibration levels bond closer, and those whose frequencies do not match distance themselves from each other in time. This is the reason we tend to strike an instant connection with some people who become a part of our life for keeps; however, some just drift away with time. Universe manifests what is meant for us by rearranging situations and circumstances in its own mysterious ways. Thus, to match the vibration of the universal energy, we need to elevate the spiritual health of mind, body, and soul.

Be Open to Receive

The universe has an abundance of everything you can ask for. Its doors are always open for you, any time and every time. It is for you to reach out to the universe through thought power and ask for what you want, with clear intent. Before you ask, you need to declare yourself to be open to receive what the universe will bestow upon you. This is the basic principle of spiritual healing. Being open means clearing your emotional and mental blockages, keeping faith in the universal life force energy, and welcoming it with open arms. *When you surrender to the universe without afterthought, the universe takes charge of you and sets you free.* Release all your stress, fears and anxieties, empty your mind, and keep it open to receive love, peace, and light.

Believe and Trust

Keeping faith and trusting and believing in anything that you do wins half the battle. This trio raises your vibrations and enhances your connectivity and receptiveness to the frequency of the universe. Make them an integral part of your life and experience the magic of how the universe conspires to make things happen for you. Trust the plan of the universe; let it roll out on its own. *An instinct is a signal from the universe. It prepares you for the unknown.* Trust your instincts. They are seldom wrong. Stop chasing and waiting for what you want. Believe it is yours, and trust that the universe will give it to you if it's meant for you. Keep this mindset, and you will never be disappointed. *Believe that everything happens for a reason, and trust that the universe knows the reason, and so it is.*

The Universe Is You

There are different truths, myths, beliefs, and studies by the experts about the universe, its origin and its mysteries. The universe is not just cosmic energy or a defined space where planets reside. It's the magical space of energy, where our thoughts travel and are refined and manifested back to reality. Our thoughts are in constant communication with the universe, which is within us. We receive the right responses if we ask the right questions. The universe emits back the same emotion we give. Sometimes we go through certain phases in life. These may seem tough and perplex us with their existence. But someday, when the plan unfolds, you will realize that it was meant to be as a part of the bigger picture of what the universe planned just for you. *Believe in yourself and so will the universe.*

The Universe Is Your Genie

Believe in yourself and trust in your capabilities and abilities to energize your thought power and to elevate your vibrational energy within and around you. This, in turn, will activate the universal energy to bring life to your thoughts. *The universal life force energy within you is your genie, which fulfills all your wishes as the lamp of your soul is caressed with love and intent.* Be a soulful person, full of positivity, purity, empathy, gratitude, and love. This will always keep you at a higher spiritual frequency as you become conscious of the thoughts you choose and the choices you make. Enjoy your present moment by keeping the genie alive within you to make your dreams come true.

> Believe in yourself and so will the universe.

Do Not Question, Just Think

When your thoughts flow easily and positively, without any blockages from doubts and reasoning, they bring the desired outcome at the required place and time. Logical reasoning is practical and resourceful. However, it is sometimes good to let go of rigid thoughts and explore the infinite possibilities that the universe has in store for us. Add some thrill to your life, and trust that the universe will give you only what is good and best for you. *Believe in the magic of the universe!*

I Am Possible

Nothing is impossible. Your thoughts have the power to create your destiny. It is up to you to take a step forward and make things happen for you. If you sit back and expect things to work out without any effort, you are setting yourself up to fail. You have to believe in yourself and set yourself up to win. *Take risks, always try, give it your best shot, and never give up. Live with a "Yes" attitude.* You do not always get what you want, but at least you get the satisfaction of having made an attempt, which is better than the guilt of not having tried.

Infinite and Unlimited

The universe and its energy stretch beyond space and time, always in abundance.

We need to tap its unlimited resources and enrich our lives. For this, we need to look beyond what eyes can see, to stretch our arms to embrace infinite possibilities in our lives and let our thoughts travel where man cannot. With love in our hearts and gratitude in every breath we take, the universe will shelter and protect us on our life's pathway. The universe is by your side. Feel and cherish its presence and be illuminated in its gift of light. Think abundantly to seek abundance in your life. Let your imagination post many thoughts into the infinite universe and bring in untold happiness, love, health, wealth, and prosperity. Lead a life full of contentment and accomplishment.

Secrets to Experience Magic of the Universe

With clear intent, post a thought into the universe for your most cherished wish. Believe this wish has been fulfilled, keep watering this thought with the power of intent and see it happen.

If you want to experience the magic of love, first love yourself and give love without any expectation. Love will come into your life in unexpected ways and fill your life with abundance.

If there is something you want in life but it seems practically impossible for you, first stop limiting your thoughts and doubting yourself. Get rid of those uncertain thoughts, and start visualizing the occurrence of what you want, however difficult it may seem. Believe it has happened and feel happy, as you would when it really does happen, and so it will be. Enjoy this game of thought creation with a winning attitude. You will succeed in whatever you do.

> Write your own story, and hold the pen for others to write theirs.

Celebrate Life

Live your present moment. Celebrate it as if there is no tomorrow. Each day you wake up to is a blessing. Add festive colors to your life without any occasion or reason. Make each day a special day. You are the universe, and you are in abundance at all given times. You have access to more than you can imagine. Match your frequency to the universe and be empowered with happiness and glory. Feel it, share it, and spread it. *Write your own story, and hold the pen for others to write theirs.* Spreading smiles is a celebration in itself. Do not waste time pondering over your past or being anxious over the future; instead, seize the moment. It's yours. Look for happiness, contentment, and joy in every situation and every relationship. Do whatever makes you happy, even if it means being weird and odd and so not you. Keep the vibrations good and attract positivity. *Be a good host, with a WELCOME ABOARD sign to bring in more and more people to celebrate with you.*

CHAPTER 9

HEAL THE WORLD

*E*nergize your being, and be a messenger of love, peace, and compassion. Establish humanity as one religion, and empower the world with positive virtues and vibrations.

Elevation of Thought

When we are in awareness of our thoughts and feelings and are working on them consciously to make a difference to ourselves and our surroundings, we are heading in the direction of thinking beyond our personal space. We are now keeping in mind the bigger picture, even while we think about the smallest things in life. Our horizons widen, and we start realizing that whatever we think and do affects not just us but the people we are associated with and, in turn, those they are connected with, and the chain continues. This affects our decision-making power, our reactions to situations and our relationships with people. *Elevation of thought is a shift of thought from I to we.*

Follow the Guiding Light

The universe has its own ways of cautioning us and guiding us. We need to follow the cues and proceed accordingly. However, very often, due to our own mental blockages and oversight, we tend to ignore these hints and miss the bus. Thus, it's important for us to be in sync with the universe and decode its secret messages at the right time. The universe offers us ample opportunities. We need to identify and act upon them. Our guardian angels are watching over us and lighting the path we need to tread upon.

> Elevation of thought is a shift of thought from I to we.

Energize Your Being

You first need to have it in you, so you can give and share. Tap the available resources in the universe, in nature and in your own thought power to enhance your inner strength. Be buoyant, with a positive frame of mind. Surround yourself with people, thoughts, and activities that elevate your vibrational frequency. Love yourself, love your body, and have a sense of belonging to where you are and where you want to be. Detoxify your mind, body, and soul with nourishing food, a balanced diet, practicing silence, and yoga. Be a livewire of positive energy who charges the spirit and brings joy into the life of all those you connect with.

Heal Yourself

Your health is in your mind. If you think you are healthy, so it is. Often we find ourselves complaining about aches and pains when our mind is idle and we have nothing else to concentrate on. Our focus is centered around our pain and suffering, which manifests into reality, as we ourselves are giving energy to the thought of pain. On the other hand, when we ignore the pain and concentrate on work or something that occupies our thoughts and mind, the energy flows there, and we do not seem to be aware of our pain and suffering; eventually, it ceases to exist.

Unhealthy thoughts lead to illness, which is the root cause of all diseases. Thoughts of well-being keep us healthy and glowing. We have the capacity to change our focus to thoughts that bring in positive energy, to feel and believe that we are in the pink of health. We have the ability to understand our body clock and make the necessary changes in our thought pattern, food intake, and lifestyle. *Self-heal with mind power.*

> The universe speaks to us; listen carefully.

Identify Your Life Purpose

Life without a purpose is like a journey without an itinerary or a roadmap. "Who am I?" and "What is the purpose of my life?" are common questions that most of us ask ourselves at some point in our lives. The answers are within us all the time, but either we do not look for them or we do not have the ability to see them clearly, as our vision is blurred. If we are observant of the hints that lead us to the journey we need to take, we will work towards it effectively and achieve what is meant for us in life. Each of us has some role to play. All we need to do is pause to observe, feel, and think. *The universe speaks to us; listen carefully.*

Global Cleansing

Cleansing the globe is clearing the dust of negativities from the globe and refilling it with energy and light. It involves cleansing the souls and the environment. It includes settling one's karmic accounts. A good cleansed soul thinks and feels good. It is an abundance of love and gratitude. It has the power to heal itself and the world. Vibrations of the soul affect the vibrations of the globe and vice versa. The first step to evolve a change at the macro level is to begin with yourself. As is said, "Charity begins at home." Hence, regular detoxification of ourselves is essential, which in turn will have a ripple effect and help to maintain the equilibrium of the life force energy.

Planting Positive Virtues

If we want our world to be a better place to live in, full of happiness and peace, we need to work on the very foundation, the root level, of the souls who influence the health of the world. We need to plant the seeds of positive virtues like love, humanity, and courage in the soul by spreading knowledge and awareness of its consciousness and effects on our life, at the personal and global levels. This needs to be supported with continued watering of its significance in our life to retain the longevity of its existence. Practical knowledge and experience of its effects have a much more profound impact than theory and notes. *You will be a true soul charger when the souls charged by you have attained the knowledge and power to charge more souls.*

Create Awareness of the Power of the Universe

When we take charge of our life by controlling and monitoring our thoughts and adjusting them to the frequency of the universe, we have the power to move the world. However, most people are ignorant of this truth or unwilling to learn and try something new. It is the moral responsibility of every good soul to spread the knowledge we have and to help others to experience this magic of the universe to transform their lives to abundance. As it is said that your responsibility does not end by taking the thirsty horse to the pond; you also have to make him drink. In doing so, you not only contribute to the betterment of the world but also attract blessings from as many lives as you touch.

Be a Messenger of Love, Peace, and Compassion

What is the first thought that comes to your mind when you think of a dove? A white bird that emits peace and purity? A symbol of compassion and a messenger of love? *Be a dove. Gather a fleet and travel all over the globe to spread the message of love, peace, and compassion.* As souls receive this message and imbibe it, it will enhance the vibrational energy of the individual and eventually his or her surroundings, and have a global effect as it matches with the frequency of the universe.

> Humanity is a relationship builder; it touches the sentiments of the person.

Establish Humanity as a Code of Conduct

Humanity is the prudent way we humans should think and behave, in our best interest and the society around us. It means respect for each other's emotions and well-being.

All the coveted titles of education and professional achievements are reduced to zero if one lacks basic humanity in thought and approach in life. We need to be conscious of imbibing humanity in our thought, actions and deeds, and in our day-to-day life. *Humanity is a relationship builder; it touches the sentiments of the person* and can bring about significant impact and changes in our personal and professional lives.

Kindle the Flame of Unity at All Levels

With love in our heart, peace in our soul, and kindness in our actions and deeds, we have the power to influence the thoughts and cleanse the souls. *When love becomes the basic language we speak, harmony the most melodious music we hear, and peace the attire we wear, all the walls of caste, creed, and religious biases will crumble.* Soul consciousness will establish uniformity and oneness among all forms of creation. *When there is no reason to compete, compare, and conflict, more souls will connect, and more hands will join to help and heal.*

Enhance the Vibrations of the Globe

Just as a tiny flame is sufficient to ignite a profound fire, so you, as a pure soul with good intentions, have the capacity to spread love and good vibrations in the world around you. All you need to do is start with your own home: A warm smile to your immediate family members every morning, a polite *thank you* to the chauffeur who helps open the car door, a gentle tap on a colleague's shoulder to wish him or her a good day all create a chain reaction of goodness. Your smile full of gratitude, your appreciation of someone's routine effort, your concern for a colleague's well-being may just trigger a feeling of happiness and joy within them. Maybe their anger might melt, or their bad day may seem better. They, in turn, will be nice to other people they come across, thus starting a chain reaction. A good deed on your end will set the ball rolling and create a multitude of good vibrations at various levels. An environment full of nature's goodness and pure vibrations from our souls will surely contribute to a healthier, happier, and more content world. We cannot change the entire world in a day or even a year. But if each individual makes an effort to at least do this much, in no time the little blue planet will experience a paradigm shift and become a more humane place to live.

Help the Creator Reform the World

Every living being that transcends into the world arrives with inherent positive virtues. However, with the passage of time, most lose the original essence. To reset the world back to where it was, the Supreme Power needs support from us souls. *We need to build an army of powerful souls to fight against all negativities and protect the line of control.* We need to undertake responsibility for opening every closed door and lighting every dark path with the necessary knowledge and awareness to change and reform thoughts and action for a blessed life and world.

Empower the World with Positive Vibrations

Energy plays a vital role in our lives. When we are depleted off positive energy due to various internal and external factors, we lose our equilibrium and feel weak. We get back to being our normal selves only after we regain the energy from the efforts we put in to restore it. In the same way, when negativity exceeds positivity there tends to be an imbalance of energy in our world. When this happens, unwelcome and unannounced natural calamities, man-made disasters, and disharmony come. However, we have the power to change the situation by increasing the vibration of the world. Factors affecting its vibrational frequency are the inhabitant souls, the thoughts they emit, the impact and effect of the activities they indulge in, and their interference with nature. We can correct this by charging more and more souls, as we have learned in the previous chapters, who will help enhance the positive vibrations in our world by instilling positive virtues among one and all and invoking spiritual energy from the Divine with regular prayers and group meditations that send out collective positive frequencies into the world.

Refine, Refresh, and Revamp the World

If each one of us feels a sense of belonging and responsibility towards the world we reside in, we will make an effort to make it a better place. Just as we feel the need to de-clutter our thoughts and homes at regular intervals to restore sanity, make room for the free flow of positive energy, and add newness and freshness to it, the world too needs a periodic cleansing, rejuvenation, and facelift to be an energized and beautiful place for all forms of existence. This can be done by strengthening and restoring love, peace, and harmony in the world by being a soul charger.

INTERVIEWS

Thoughts shared by **Mrs. Roop Lakhani**
Author of the limited-edition book
The Inner Journey **and upcoming book** *Mind Seeds*
Coach, Consultant, Trainer, Healer

- Soul Healing ∗ Radical Healing ∗ Theta Healing ∗ Integrated Healing
- Journey Healing of Mind and Emotions ∗ Certified Practitioner of Access Bars
- Tarot Card Reading ∗ Runes Reading ∗ Tea Leaf Reading ∗ Numerology ∗ Graphology
- Matrix Reimprinting ∗ YUEN ∗ EFT ∗ Psych K ∗ NLP Coaching ∗ Vaastu Shastra
- Hypnotherapy ∗ Past Life Regression

Address: Siddhagiri, 18th A Rd, Mumbai, Maharashtra 400052, Khar West, Mumbai, Maharashtra 400052
Email: roop@tarotfuture.com
Cell: +91 98 2161 2031
Webpages: www.TarotFuture.com, www.RoopLakhani.co.in, www.UnlimitAccess.com

Q. After having practiced various techniques of alternate healing for almost two decades, what are your thoughts on soul healing and any of the topics covered in The Soul Charger?

Soul Healing

A soul is a tiny, sentient, metaphysical point of spiritual light. Light means knowledge. The inherent nature of a soul is love, peace, harmony, and oneness. The human body is a complex pattern of physical energies and complex mind. It has come to enjoy materialistic desires. But when the mind takes excessive control over thoughts, feelings, and behavior of body consciousness and its excessive desires and ego, then it gives rise to lust, anger, greed, ego, and attachments, which create suffering. Unless the heart does not become a spiritual heart and strike a balance between the spiritual activity and materialistic activity, the soul is not at rest. **The keys to soul healing are self -awareness and self-realization.** When we try to know our inner self (soul) with our self (mind) and finally become one with the universal soul, we are blessed with the self-knowledge, or self-realization, that leads to true enlightenment towards *Sat-chit-ananda*; that is, truth, peace, and bliss.

Human beings are infinite beings of light, capable of spreading the light with their own light. The *soul-ar* light is luminated with solar light, which is symbolic of optimism, positivity, and freshness. It is time to love and accept ourselves and others unconditionally and avoid looking beyond the walls of judgment, separation, and past hurts. Each one of us has to be standing in true power and authenticity to declare, "I am the light"; then the light would be there to make each one of us light. Declare, "I am love," and the world will be a loving heaven to stay in. The divinity lies in each one's heart and soul.

Attitude of Gratitude

Gratitude improves psychological health, reduces toxic emotions, and increases happiness, love, and harmony.

The first gratitude goes to the Creator for gifting us such a beautiful soul, mind, and body. The second gratitude goes to our parents, who brought us on this physical Earth. The third gratitude goes to the Sun, the water, the wind, space, and the Earth. Without their graceful unending energies, we would not have been able to exist. We can be grateful to all the flora, fauna, and life existing on this earth, on which we are completely dependent. We can be grateful to every human being for their contributions, creation, and generative capacities. The last, and not the least, gratitude goes to each one's divinity inside for the brilliance and magnificence it holds inside that allows each one of us to be a part of the consciousness towards love, peace, and harmony. **My energy equation is E = M x C x C, where E is energy, M is mind, C is consciousness and C the is choices we make.** Life is all about what consciousness and choice we make through our mind, and the loving energies emerge beautifully.

The Magic of the Universe

There are 100 billion neurons in the body: 100,000,000,000. Our mind includes the whole universe. We have 37.2 trillion cells, and they all work with each other in harmony to keep us going. This proves that we are the magical creation of the magical universe. The human population of the universe is only 7.6 billion. We are a micro part of the macro universe, or cosmos. The universe is part of All That Is, which is the same as the Divine Power that lies at our spiritual heart. We all are Divine light beings, vibrating at certain frequencies that stem from our thoughts and feelings. Let us all vibrate with the frequency of love, peace, and harmony.

Food for Thought

Thoughts create your reality, and emotions create your vibrations. Your perceptions and interpretations of events are the facets of your thoughts that either create a life worth living or a life worth miseries, so mindfully mind the mind. Use God-gifted intuition, willpower, and right intellect to see the unseen mysteries of life towards self-understanding and oneness.

Health Is a State of Mind

Seventy percent of health problems are due to psychosomatic stress, worries, and emotional clutter. **The wonderful magic drug called the "Mind" can solve our mental, emotional, and physical health issues**. Self-care and deep healing through mindfulness are the keys to an easy life. The Mind is the tool to address all problems of life; hence, we need to heal the mind and bridge the gaps between soul, mind, and body.

Thoughts shared by **Mrs. Sunita Singad**
India's first qualified Angel Therapy practitioner,
certified by Doreen Virtue in 2005
Life coach

First Indian breath practitioner, certified by Gay and Katie Hendricks
Qualified teacher /trainer by Louise Hay
Co-author of the book *A Walk with the Angels*

Email: sunitasingad@hotmail.com
Cell: + 91 98 3392 8100
Webpage: www.earthangels.in

Q. What is Angelic Reading? Your thoughts on Spirit of Love?

Angels are beings of light. They come from the essence of love.

Most of us think of angels in a particular form that is easy to visualize. However, in reality, they are flashes of light and have no specific form. We call them to ease our lives.

Angels help iron out the problems for us. They reduce the impact. Sometimes they even aid in instant healing. There are two guardian angels (one on your left side and one on your right). They are with us through our lifetime. *However, they communicate with us only through free will.* If we do not call them, they do not come. The essence is that we have to call them; we have to ask them what we need to know.

While there are various tools to connect to your angels, Sunita implements trance channeling using the medium of oracle cards for angel reading sessions. One or more sessions are held by the practitioner with the one who seeks guidance. Questions are asked to angels, and guidance is provided as per the intuitive responses sought by the angelic readers.

The universe says to use its available abundant resources. Be in the present. Connect with the universe and your angels by being an embodiment of love. *Love is the language of the angels.*

Open yourself. Connect and communicate with them with your thought power. Ask them to bless you with a better, healthy life. Once you have finally opened yourself up and asked, you have opened the door for a big shift based on the fundamental of love.

How will you experience the presence/effect of the connection with unseen divine angels in your life?

When you establish a connection with your guardian angels, you sense a good feeling within you. Deep down in your heart, your anxiety levels will drop, and your emotional pain will reduce. You will start taking better care of yourself. Your external support system will be autoactivated, and you might meet new people to give you the wisdom to help you get ready to face the challenges life has in store for you. You may be attracted to or gifted a book or literature that is meant to be a guiding source of light for you to tread upon. You will also notice that, all of a sudden, you will start becoming aware and appreciative of the beauty and bounty of nature, and material comforts and luxuries take a back seat. You start feeling the space God has created for you. All that the angels ask is to send gratitude from the space where you were to the space you have now reached.

A simple technique to connect to angels.

Whenever you feel disillusioned by a challenge or simply upset, visualize the color pink, the color of love, surrounding your being from head to toe, and inhale this color deeply. Continue this slow and easy-paced breath for approximately five minutes, and feel the love energy flow through you as a blessing from the angels above. The possibility of you feeling at ease and relaxed after this process is very high.

Thoughts shared by **Mr. Indroneel Chatterjee**
Honorary Research Associate and Lecturer at
Oxford Brookes University
Lecturing undergraduates in International
Marketing and post-graduates
in Consumer Behavior.

Ongoing PhD, MSc. PG Cert, BMM.
Oxford Face of the Year 2014 at Oxford Fashion Week, UK.
Model at Sandra Reynold Agency, UK

Email: indroneelchatterjee@gmail.com
Facebook Page: www.facebook.com/leoneil.chats?ref=br_rs
Twitter: neil_chats

Q. Since your academic and professional interest deals with understanding
human behavior and attitudes, please share your thoughts on the same.
Also, what, according to you, would be the shift of thought to have an SQ
(spiritual quotient)?

To understand why people behave the way they do, we need to probe
into the minds of individuals and find out the trigger points that
actually translate their attitude into behavior. Mindsets of people have
changed. Most of us feel abundant with materialistic possessions,
rather than simplicity.

One should not be overwhelmed by emotions and should keep
going. When life is moving at its own pace and time, with so many
occurrences and ups and downs, consider yourself to be a spectator in
the middle. Focus on simplicity. Choose to observe. Think of practical
solutions. **No melodrama.**

Listen to listen; do not listen to reply. People do not listen to you. They want to express and end up speaking over you most of the time. Love—it is not just romance. It's a bonding, a connection, that can exist between you and nature, between you and an object, or between two or more individuals. However, when most of us fall in love with someone, we invest all our concentration and energies on that one person and ignore the rest. Thus, the fate of this one relationship affects our overall emotions and our health, making us feel unstable.

If we spread the fragrance of love to one and all, one drop that evaporates would not empty the ocean. Another thought on reacting to people or judging them: *We should try and base our judgment on the intent, rather than observed behavior.* Most of us focus on what's going on superficially rather than deconstruct the underpinnings of why someone behaves the way they do. There is almost always a cognitive explanation.

Try meditation. It does not have to be a serious or planned process. *It is anything and everything you can do to relax your mind.* It helps you stay in control of yourself. Meditation is to be done neutrally, without expectations. If you approach meditation with certain expectation, you are already stressing yourself with the end goal! It never is about the end goal; it is about being at peace with the journey.

So if I were to recommend a shift in thought, it would definitely be dropping the belief that materialistic acquisition and happiness are positively correlated! The pursuit of happiness is a lot simpler—it's relationships and experiences.

Thoughts shared by **Mrs. Radha Thakur**
Tarot card reader and workshops

Office Address: 236, 2nd Floor, Hub Town Solaris, Andheri (E), Mumbai
Cell: +91 98 7000 6668
Email: radhathakur46@gmail.com
Facebook page: journeywithtarotcardsandme

Q. What is Tarot card reading in a nutshell?

Tarot cards are alive. They speak the language of the universe. They give you the answers you need. However, your questions need to be clear. *Clarity of thought is of utmost importance.* There are 98 Tarot cards (22 Major and 76 Minor). Each card has a story to tell, a message to give. Each Minor card has one or more of four symbols that resonate with four elements (Wands: Fire), (Pentacles: Earth), (Cups: Water) and (Swords: Air). Major cards have no elements. In Tarot reading, the Tarot reader helps the client handle the present well, with guidance and self-realization regarding what the drawn cards have to say about the questions asked. However, the client needs to make an effort to work on his or her thoughts, with the guidance sought and mirror shown, to make things happen for them.

What are your thoughts on a few of the topics covered in
The Soul Charger: *Namely Thought Creates Destiny, Attitude of*
Gratitude and Magic of the Universe?

- Thought is a seed. What you sow, so shall you reap. Be very careful of the power of intent and power of thought. If you sow the right seed of thought, negative thoughts or evil eye will not exist in your universe. Make your aura so strong that nothing can touch or enter it.

- *The Mind is a monkey. What you feed it, it manifests.*

- *Ho'oponopono* is a well-known Hawaiian healing technique from Dr. Ihaleakala Hew Len. It follows a simple method of creating four thoughts in your mind in any sequence for healing any given situation or for any person close or distant: "I am sorry," "Please forgive me," "I love you," and "Thank you."

- ***What comes to you easily is what is meant to be.*** The Almighty does not want you to chase after anything. He effortlessly and easily gives you what is good for you. Thus, if we find ourselves chasing or running after someone or something with renewed effort, it's probably because we are working against the will of the universe.

Thoughts shared by **Mrs. Suchhanda**
Interior Designer (created more than
125 restaurants and office spaces)
Storyteller, Scriptwriter for the movie *Un-kahi*

Email: meenoo09@gmail.com
Cell: +91 98 2102 3683

Q. *What does soul charging mean to you? Share your thoughts on topics covered in* The Soul Charger.

Happiness is meditation. Even 30 seconds of meditation can spark happiness within us.

Laughter is the key to happiness and the medicine for all ailments of the body and soul.

When you laugh, your thoughts slow down. When you cry, your thoughts increase. Adding a comic element or a sense of humor in all that you think and do changes the vibration of your feelings and purifies the environment. Children are so full of life, and they laugh so easily over the silliest and most insignificant things in life, emitting positive energy in and around them. We love having them around us as they make us feel good. Can we not enliven the child within us and make ourselves and others around feel good?

Laughter is the purest source of oxygen.

Make laughter a part of your healthy daily diet. Get into the habit of laughing at every situation, anytime and every time. Express it without an afterthought. Its okay if people think you're crazy. They may mock you and gossip about you, but while thinking of you or your silliness, if they are in good spirits and laughing or smiling, you have actually contributed to energizing their souls with positivity.

Soul resides in your body. The health of soul reflects the health of the body. If your soul is happy, your body is happy. Also, when you are happy, the environment becomes happy too.

Accept the best and worst situations that come into your life. Do not crib or moan. *Just say to yourself, It's okay.* In fact, tell the universe, *"Give me all my share of sorrows now. I will handle it, overcome it, and be ready to welcome happy times ahead."* Keep your focus on the good that is on its way as you wade through the hurdles, stepping stones to the pathways of happiness and bliss, and so will it be. Think and believe that every event and occurrence in your life is orchestrated by the universe. You cannot avoid it or escape it. Do not question it; just manage it. *Manage the environment that is gifted to you.* When it's time for you to be happy, you will be. *First Bhog, then Tyaag:* That is, first enjoy the taste of life, experience its joys and sorrows until the point of saturation, and then sacrifice if and what you feel like leaving behind as you find and pursue the purpose of your life.

When we concentrate our energies on our problems and sufferings, compete and compare, with thoughts of "Why me?" our sadness intensifies and has a lingering effect on us and the surroundings we live in. *We must accept the fact that change is constant. Nothing lasts forever. We need to let go and move on.* That is the only correct thing to do.

Be a forgiver. Be strong. Be happy. Look at each soul as an equal. *Learn. Unlearn. Relearn.*

Thoughts shared by **Dr. Sunil S Harlalkaa**
Land healer and Vastu consultant

Website: www.perfectvastu.in
Facebook Page: www.facebook.com/sunil.harlalkaa /
www.facebook.com/PerfectVastuConsultancy
LinkedIn: www.linkedin.com/in/sunilharlalkaa
Email: drsunil@perfectvastu.in

Q. What are your thoughts on soul charging?

The objective of soul charging is to connect and communicate easily with the universal life-force energy.

We feel the need to charge our cellphone: ***We want to communicate. We want to connect.*** Similarly, the soul needs to be charged on a regular basis to establish a connection with the divine energy in order to communicate effortlessly with the universal life force energy.

The frequency and duration of soul charging changes from person to person. However, in the present times, our soul needs to be charged on a daily basis at frequent intervals to keep the battery charged and ever ready to function.

The Vibrations of the soul: Everything in the universe vibrates at a particular frequency.

A radio transmitter has different music or news channels attributed to different frequencies. We can switch to the channel of our choice only by tuning in to the appropriate frequency.

Astonishing Fact and Belief

When two people catch a cold at the same time, we blame it on the virus. However, it is believed that two known people can catch a cold at the same time despite being distant, only because their emotions and thoughts are at same level of frequency at a given point in time.

De-clutter. When we de-clutter our home or clean our wardrobe, we feel lighter. Why?

Everything in the universe has energy and vibrations. Energy affects your mind, body, spirit, and soul. Empty space is required for the movement of all the elements in nature.

Physically, we are cleaning the house, disposing off unwanted material objects. In doing so, **we are emitting our choice to the universe of what we want to keep and what we want to let go**. But, in essence, we are actually creating space to refill with new positive energy by de-cluttering our thoughts and clearing the dust off our emotions. Although our efforts to de-clutter are on a physical level, it's actually a spiritual transgression. As there is newness in the environment, there is newness in thoughts and emotions.

Practical Example to Gauge Negative Energy

Take a tour of your home and check the corners. Wherever you find cold or dampness, that corner is filled with toxic energy, as energy is stuck to produce negativity. You can change the energy to positive by de-cluttering that area and creating warmth in that corner by lighting a lamp.

Thoughts shared by **Master Vedant Malik**
Five-year-old pure and divine soul

Hobbies: Painting, arts and crafts
Email: vedantmalik7@gmail.com

Vedant is a creative child, good at arts and crafts. He has gifted me with many of his paintings since childhood as he is a generous child. His painting, included in this book, is his interpretation of The Soul Charger. When asked to depict it, the impromptu responses received from him urged me to take his interview and share the pure and divine thoughts of this little soul with you.

Q. Vedant, I am writing a book called The Soul Charger. **Can you make a spiritual painting for me that I can include in my book, which will be in it for life?**

He immediately said, "I need to think," and pondered for a while. Then, after a few minutes, he quipped, "I know what I am going to draw. I am going to draw a magnet," and he made the painting above in five minutes, without any help or cues from anyone.

Why did you think of drawing a magnet?

A magnet will pull everything towards the earth. So God can use all His powers again. So He does not need to go out and get power. He only needs to get power from the magnet souls.

But why does God need to get power?

God needs power so that instead of bad things coming, good things will happen. All those people who do bad things will vanish away, and only good things will come.

But why does God need to pull powerful souls with a magnet?

So that God gets the power. Otherwise, how will he help all those other people who are in trouble?

What does the book The Soul Charger **mean?**

The soul charger means solving the problems of the soul.

Where does God stay? And how can we reach him from the Earth?

God stays above in clouds. There is a staircase to reach God. It has a rope of the soul charger that God pulls from the clouds from one end, and the other end of the rope is on the Earth. The souls from Earth can hold on to this rope and climb the staircase to reach God. *The soul charger is the rope on the staircase by which you can reach God from the Earth through the dark clouds.* There are many stars in the sky, but there is one bright star in the clouds close to where God stays, and it's shooting light to the earth, and that is why there is a lot of light on the Earth.

Why is God up and not down?

God is up because when bad things happen on Earth, then the power just comes down instead of God. It comes down just before the bad things come, like a shooting star, as that is where it belongs. But He cannot come back again soon, as He lives very far, at the edge of the moon. There is a staircase that goes up to his house. This staircase has 100 steps. *God's house is red in color. However, he loves all the rainbow colors.*

If someone reads your interview in my book and wants to meet you, and asks me, "Who is this child?" what should I say to them?

Tell them I am the Magnet Boy because I am a magnet.

ABOUT THE AUTHOR

Archana Dhurandhar is a career professional with a passion for creative writing, as well as an avid reader of spiritual books. As part of her current assignment, she spearheads the e-commerce division of a leading diamond jewelry export organization in Mumbai. During her academic years, she was the recipient of multiple praises and appreciation for excellence in creative writing and literature. Albeit unpublished to date, Search for Excellence was her first spiritual article, written more than two decades ago, inspired by the preaching of Late Shri Dattapadma Swami, a spiritual guru. This sowed the seeds of Archana's first book, *The Soul Charger*.

This was followed by her association with Eckaankur Holistic Centre where she learned Reiki and The Brahmakumaris World Spiritual University for learning the art of Rajyoga Meditation, which has made a gradual shift in her thought patterns and redefined her life's purpose. Glimpses of their soul-churning principles and teachings are reflected in *The Soul Charger*. She firmly believes her book is a blessing of the Divine, meant to spread the elusive secret of celebrating life to mankind. She intends to continue writing more soul churning books and to establish herself as a holistic/ motivational speaker, in the pursuit of touching more souls and spreading more light.

Archana Dhurandhar is a finely balanced, compassionate, empathetic person. Blessed with a magnetic personality and a charming smile, she radiates positivity wherever she treads and leaves an indelible impression on all those she comes in contact with. She is charismatic, a confidante, and an anchor to many. She embarked on her spiritual quest after an anxious childhood battling recurring visions and vivid dreams of her past life. The seeds of her pathway to connect with the Divine were sown when she suffered from a severe health breakdown, the time when she turned to the Rajyoga Meditation of The Brahmakumaris. Ardent practice transformed her, and she recuperated and regained her emotional and physical well-being. Archana shares her insights and soul-empowering knowledge through personal experience to help you connect and reconnect with life and the Divine with *The Soul Charger*.

ECKAANKUR WHOLISTIC HEALING

Mrs. Anjali Sengupta

Certified Reiki Master, Pranic Healer, Integrated Clinical Hypnotherapist, Metaphor Therapist, Access Bars Therapist Mumbai, Maharashtra

Email: enjoliesen@gmail.com

Cell# +91 9819964721

Fb Page: *www.facebook.com/eckaankur.wholistichealing/about*

Gratitude is a positive emotion. It assists in chasing away the toxicity and accepts happiness.

IdoThankU is here to make your choice in leading a grateful life easier. As leaders of this initiative, they aim to change individuals, by ensuring gratitude awareness. Its benefits ranging from physical, mental, emotional and professional.

One of the services provided is gratitude workshops, leading to increased co-operation and collaboration of the companies with others, ensuring a smooth relationship within itself and the employees. Enhanced performance is seen. Gratitude within the company ensures positivity of the employees as well as the atmosphere.

A happy employee is a vital asset for a company's success. IdoThankU has inculcated gratitude in companies such as Indian Oil; Our 'ThankU' cards were used by Famous Marathi Play 'Ke Dil Abhi Bhara Nahi' to express gratitude to its audience and by Tata Memorial Hospital to its donors and volunteers.

Gratitude can be expressed on an individual, social, corporate, educational level through our services.

"If you want to find Happiness, find gratitude."

IdoThankU is the perfect choice towards showcasing your gratitude. Practicing Gratitude is vital and IdoThankU provides variety of services for corporate, schools and individuals. Begin your journey today! Go the IdoThankU way.

Mother's Day

Idothanku took an initiative to express gratitude to Mothers

Transgender Empowerment

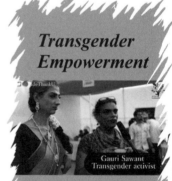

Gauri Sawant
Transgender activist

Transgenders expressed gratitude to the people through IdoThankU who came out to support them

Few Clients Served

Indian Oil

Plays

Tata Memorial

 / **IdoThankU** | ⊕ **www.idothanku.com** | Contact Us : 9820245056
connect@idothanku.com

SPECIAL THANKS

SPECIAL THANKS TO MY WELL—WISHERS
FOR THEIR ENCOURAGEMENT, LOVE & SUPPORT
IN THE MAKING OF *THE SOUL CHARGER*

LATA & SHRIKANT RANE	ROMA & PUNEET MALIK
MANGALA & SURESH JAYAKAR	Dr. PAVAN & PRANJAL KIRTIKAR
SHEILA AJINKYA	Dr. SHILPA JAYAKAR
SHEFALI & SUHAS AJINKYA	ASHISH & SHABANA AJINKYA
RUPALI AJINKYA	KRANTI KULKARNI
NAVIN SADARANGANI	UDAYRAJ GADNIS
SHITAL SHAH	SUNALI THAKKAR
SANCHITA CHATTERJEE	SUCHHANDA CHATTERJEE
BHAVESH RAJGOR	NAINA GIYANANI
RAHUL LOTLIKAR	HEMANT PANPALIA
JAISON THAMBI	SURESH MAHESHWARI
LALIT RATHI	LAHOTI VIKAS
NITA SHINDE	SAMITA BANERJEE

OTHER BOOKS RECOMMENDED BY BLACK CARD BOOKS

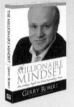

The Millionaire Mindset
*How Ordinary People Can
Create Extraordinary Income*
Gerry Robert
ISBN: 978-1-927411-00-1

**Publish a Book &
Grow Rich**
*How to Use a Book as
a Marketing Tool &
Income Accelerator*
Gerry Robert
ISBN: 978-1-77204-546-8

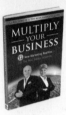

Multiply Your Business
*10 New Marketing Realities
for the Real Estate Industries*
Gerry Robert &
Theresa Barnabei, DREC
ISBN: 978-1-77204-774-5

Image Power
*Balancing Passion and
Profit in Business*
David McCammon
ISBN: 978-1-77204-825-4

Your Talent Is a Gift
*How to Value Your Talents,
Your Keys to Winning
Consistently in Life!
The Road from
Talent to Success*
Ingrid M.A. Gumbs
ISBN: 978-1-927892-83-1

Sales Booster
*The New Science &
Art of Selling*
Nimesh Mehta
ISBN: 978-1-77204-622-9

**The Queen of
the Comeback**
*7 Ways For Anyone To Bounce
Back From Life's Obstacles*
Nidhika Bahl
ISBN: 978-1-77204-620-5

Lead or Bleed
*How Entrepreneurs and
Corporate Leaders Can Adopt
a Proven System to Stop Fire
Fighting and Start Accelerating
Performance And Profits*
Rajiv Talreja
ISBN: 978-1-77204-266-5

POWERED BY

www.blackcardbooks.com